QUILTER'S ACADEMY

Vol. 3—Junior Year

A Skill-Building Course in Quiltmaking

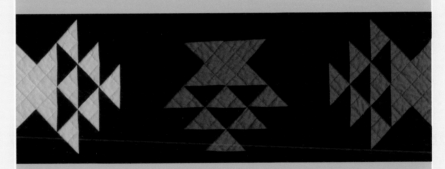

Harriet Hargrave & Carrie Hargrave

C&T PUBLISHING

Text copyright © 2011 by Harriet Hargrave and Carrie Hargrave

Artwork copyright © 2011 by C&T Publishing, Inc.

Publisher: Amy Marson

Creative Director: Gailen Runge

Acquisitions Editor: Susanne Woods

Editor: Carrie Hargrave

Book Design Director: Kristen Yenche

Cover/Book Designer: Kerry Graham

Production Coordinator: Zinnia Heinzmann

Production Editor: Alice Mace Nakanishi

Illustrator: Wendy Mathson

Photography by Christina Carty-Francis and Diane Pedersen of C&T Publishing, Inc., unless otherwise noted

Published by C&T Publishing, Inc., P.O. Box 1456, Lafayette, CA 94549

Library of Congress Cataloging-in-Publication Data

Hargrave, Harriet.

Quilter's Academy Vol 1.- Freshman Year : a skill-building course in quiltmaking / by Harriet Hargrave and Carrie Hargrave.

p. cm.

ISBN 978-1-57120-594-0 (softcover)

1. Patchwork. 2. Quilting. I. Hargrave, Carrie, 1976- II. Title.

TT835.H3384 2009

746.46--dc22

2009008787

Printed in China

10 9 8 7 6 5 4 3 2 1

A Course in Quilting

A fresh new approach to uncovering the details that make quilting fun and successful for the beginner.

Quilting 301—Junior Year

You are stepping into the exciting world of triangles and all the design possibilities that triangle units provide. Not only will you learn many different methods of making half-square triangles, but we have also added Flying Geese, three-piece and quarter-square triangles, and Feathered Stars. Along with all this, there are more internal frame ideas for you to incorporate into your quilt designs. Now the fun can really begin!

Note from the Authors

This is the third volume, and we know that we have not caught every single mistake or typo in every book before this. We don't know that it is possible to see what the fresh eyes of our readers see, or to produce a book without a couple of errors. We certainly don't know of many. From the many emails we have received now, we have come to look upon the problems as learning opportunities. Many students of these books have stated that they knew they were learning because they could spot the problem right away and knew how to correct it. Yay! That is exactly the point of these books—for you to get so knowledgeable and secure in your techniques that if you find an error, you will know how to work it out without it stopping you cold in your tracks. We appreciate your letting us know where there is an error so that we can get it corrected in the next printing.

Dedication

We dedicate this book to both Barbara Johanna and Mary Ellen Hopkins, whose ideas and influence are a big part of the content of this volume. We honor their ingenuity and inspiration.

The authors take full responsibility for the contents of this book, including the technical accuracy of the information. Please direct any questions to quilt.academy.q.a@earthlink.net. Please visit the Quilter's Academy blog, too, for additional information and discussions: quiltersacademy.blogspot.com.

Contents

Preface

You are now starting the third book in this series of six books. The purpose of the series is to build your quiltmaking skills on a firm foundation from beginner to advanced. Volumes 1 and 2 laid the foundation for all the rest of the books. Volume 1 covered basic quilts using strips and squares in a straight set. You were taught to get your accuracy and precision started. Volume 2 continued in this vein, putting blocks on point, adding settings that are more difficult, and starting the process of designing your own original quilts. If you have not worked through the first two books thoroughly, we strongly suggest that you go back and absorb the information in those books before you proceed to this one.

Each book in this series is not all-inclusive. We are putting them together as a college course, and each book builds on the previous one. Please *do not* use them as mere pattern books. You are apt to find the instructions less than complete if you have not learned the lessons from each previous book and prior to a particular pattern.

This volume will introduce you to the world of triangles. The approach is changing a bit from the first two volumes. There will be more detail on how to have total success in the piecing processes.

Introduction

Accuracy in making triangle units is mandatory if you are going to have a successful quilt. Take your time and work through each of the exercises carefully. We have given you the chance to try many different ways of making the same thing; it is up to you to decide which method makes the most sense for the project you are making. You will find there is not any one technique that is perfect for every block or pattern. We strongly recommend that you make the sampler quilt, as it uses the sample pieces you produce with each technique of half-square triangles. Doing the work is the only way to really experience the process of each technique. We will give you our ideas of the pros and cons of each technique, but the final decision is yours. They all have their assets, so try them all.

This book is much more concentrated on technique and the quilts. Harriet has written the basic instructions for each Class, but Carrie has written the detailed instructions for each of the projects. While writing this book, we found that much of what Harriet wrote was a blur to Carrie, who is learning a lot of this information just as you are. So once Harriet has taught you the basic technique, Carrie will help explain in detail what will help you be successful when constructing the quilts. *Please* read the instructions for each quilt thoroughly before starting. *Please* do the exercises before starting a project. We want you to have the best possible end result—jumping in at the middle will not help you achieve this.

We are taking you from basic quilts made with half-square triangles to Feathered Stars in this volume. Accuracy is of utmost importance. We are not pushing perfectionism but precision. The one thing that you need to keep in mind at this point is that as the techniques get more complicated or detailed, the more time it will take to make each of the projects. This is a good time to start learning to slow down and enjoy the process of making a quilt. We hope you would rather learn to make a few awesome quilts that represent excellent workmanship than many mediocre projects that are thrown together in a hurry. Make quilting what you do when you want to de-stress and relax. When you are being creative, you go to a place in your brain that does not recognize the outside world. Strive to go to that place as often as you can, and strive for excellence!

Once you have mastered triangles, Volume 4 will take you into the beautiful patterns that use 45° and 60° diamonds. The accuracy you obtain by learning triangles will lead you into set-in piecing with confidence.

—Harriet and Carrie

Class 310

If you haven't read the Preface and the Introduction preceding this Class, please go back and do so. Important information about how this book works, as well as how it fits into the series, is contained there and is vital to your knowing how to use this book.

LESSON ONE:
More tools
SEAM GUIDES

As we discussed in Volume 1 (Class 130, Lesson Two, page 22) seam guides create a "barrier" for the fabric to ride alongside of. This edge gives you something to align the fabric with while sewing. A seam guide that attaches to the bed of your machine may be the best way you could set up the barrier for accuracy: a stack of Post-it Notes, a thick piece of ¼" masking tape, a screw-on guide, and so forth. Any of these types of seam guides work great when you are stitching along the raw edges of two pieces of fabric.

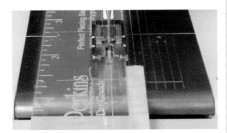

Placing tape alongside ruler

You will find, however, that some of the techniques in the lessons in this volume will require you to sew on top of the fabric alongside a marked line. If your seam guide is attached to the bed of your machine, you will have to remove it so that you can keep the fabric flat against the throat plate of the machine. Now you are going to have to use the edge of a ¼" foot, if you have one, and work with a drawn line. As you progress into the different techniques used to make half-square and quarter-square triangle units, you might want to make samples of each triangle method first to find out just where the edge of the foot or your needle needs to be placed in relation to the line. You might need to be on the left, just to the side of, or right on top of the line. This will be an individual issue for each quilter and their machine. You may find a ¼" foot with a guide blade built onto the front of the right toe helpful, as the blade can easily be placed where needed and viewed clearly as the sewing progresses. More than anything, we are going for accuracy, so whatever foot gives you the best results is the one you want to use.

Blade on foot guiding along line

When using the techniques that have drawn lines for guidance, you might find that working with a regular sewing foot works best, especially if you are working on a 9mm feed dog embroidery machine. Check the bottom of the foot to be sure that it is flat, with just a small opening right behind where the needle goes into the foot. If it is flat, it will hold the fabric firmly against the feed dogs. If you use an open-toe embroidery foot, the fabric is more likely to slip, as there is a deep groove in the bottom of the foot to accommodate satin stitching. When sewing with a drawn line, you will, in most cases, need to keep the needle just to the seam allowance side of the line, so you will need to watch the needle more than the foot. If you have wide feed dogs—9mm needle swing—you will find that the right feed dog is barely used, if at all, by the right toe of the ¼" foot. Some techniques have you sewing down the center of a square instead of along a narrow seam allowance, and the wider foot will help the fabric feed more evenly on these wide feed dogs. Use a Dremel or Wizard cutting tool to open the area just in front of the needle to give you better vision and closer control, especially if you're using a stiletto.

Using wider foot when sewing on squares with line

Sewing along a line and staying perfectly straight and accurate is not always easy. For that reason, in most of the techniques in the lessons, we have you cut the units slightly larger than is mathematically correct so the pieces can be trimmed to the exact size once they are sewn and pressed. There are a couple of techniques, however, in which exact sewing is a requirement of the process. We suggest that you try both—the techniques with mathematically correct measurements and the ones with fudge room—and see how accurate you are and which technique suits your working style.

> *tip* If you find that your pieces consistently become uneven by the end of the seam, you might need to lower the pressure on the presser foot. If you have an adjustment dial on your machine, experiment with loosening the pressure by degrees until two units come out exactly the same length.

SCISSORS

We have not discussed scissors yet. Up until now, there has been little need for them, as the fabrics have been easily cut into strips and squares using a rotary cutter. When cutting on lines used as sewing guides as well as when trimming off points, you might find it is just as quick and easy to use scissors as to use a rotary cutter. Below is some helpful information on choosing scissors.

Scissors come in different qualities and shapes for different jobs. The large dressmaking shears we generally have in our sewing baskets are not necessarily needed in quiltmaking. Smaller, lighter-weight scissors are more useful.

Fabric scissors should be able to cut through several layers of fabric all the way to the very end of the point. When trying out scissors, consider the following:

* Are they heavy in the hand or very comfortable?

* How do your fingers fit in the handle openings?

* How much control do you have when cutting around tight curves?

* How straight do they cut?

* Do they slip as they cut?

* Will the points at the very tip cut a thread of the fabric?

When shopping for scissors, ask if you can cut with them before purchasing. The scissors might be pretty in the package, but comfort and function can only be understood once they are in your hand and cutting through two to four layers of fabric. This is a very personal decision to be made without the help or suggestions of

friends and sales associates. We try to avoid carrying cheap scissors in our store, as good tools are equal to good workmanship. Consider them a long-term investment and buy the very best quality you can afford.

Various scissors

RULERS

We are introducing a few specialty rulers and tools that are required for different techniques when making triangle units. You may want to consider adding them to your collection. Trimming is involved in the techniques presented in this book, and having the right tools makes the job much easier. There are also several rulers that measure, do the math, and figure where you need to cut, all at the same time, making some techniques easier if you dislike working with math. The following list explains most of the rulers we will be working with throughout this book:

* **Judy Martin's Point Trimmer—** This is a handy tool for pretrimming the points of triangles or any 45° angles to eliminate bulk at the seams and enable easy alignment of the patches.

* **Marsha McCloskey's Precision Trimmer 6—**This is our favorite ruler for trimming and squaring after sewing and pressing half-square triangles. This ruler is unique, as it has the cut sizes printed on it so that it is easy to measure with the seam allowances added when trimming. The interior lines are

wonderful for squaring with the seams within the block.

❋ **Easy Angle**—Sharon Hultgren developed this clever ruler for cutting accurate triangles from strips. Measurements are built in for easy placement.

❋ **Bias Square ruler**—This ruler has all the lines printed in a chevron formation, making cutting squares from bias strips very easy.

❋ **Perfect Patchwork Templates by Marti Mitchell**—These laser-cut acrylic templates have the seam allowance added for accuracy. A double blunt corner system helps with perfect alignment of shapes when sewing. These are especially helpful when working with books and patterns that use templates. You don't have to make your own.

❋ **Flying Geese rulers**—There are several different ways to measure and trim Flying Geese patches. These rulers will be addressed in Class 350.

Various rulers to help with triangles of all shapes and sizes

LESSON TWO:
Review of the basics

Following is a list of the basic piecing principles that we covered in detail in Volumes 1 and 2.

❋ Always work on the straight of grain, either lengthwise or crosswise. Be sure that you have torn both ends of your yardage and have realigned the crosswise grain of all the pieces

before you begin to cut. See Volume 1, Class 120, Lesson Three (pages 16–17).

❋ Accurate cutting is the beginning of your success or frustration as you piece. Be sure to use the correct ruler for the job. You need to commit to a single brand of rulers that you can easily read to maintain accuracy. See Volume 1, Class 120, Lessons Four and Five (pages 17–19).

❋ Find your personal accurate seam allowances. Remember that ¼″ seam allowances don't work, but scant ¼″ seam allowances do. Set up a system on your machine that allows you to have accurate finished units, not perfect ¼″ seam allowances. See Volume 1, Class 130, Lessons One and Two (pages 20–23).

❋ Pressing can make or break your quilt top. Therefore, it is one of the most important processes to master. Proper pressing leads to flat, straight, extremely accurate pieced tops. If you are still working on a standard ironing board, now might be the time to invest in a Big Board or similar product. A high-quality iron such as the Reliable Digital Velocity is also helpful when pressing. See Volume 1, Class 130, Lesson Four (page 26).

❋ Trim for accuracy. After you sew and press each seam, align a ruler on the seam and check that the strip measurement from the seam to the raw edge is exact. This prevents all the small distortions that occur when cutting, sewing, and pressing. See Volume 1, Class 130, Lesson Five (page 27).

❋ Always start with a well-cleaned and oiled machine. See Volume 2, Class 210, Lesson Two (pages 6–14).

❋ Sew samples with the fabrics you are going to be using to check for thread tension problems. See Volume 2, Class 210, Lesson Two (page 11).

❋ Always start with a new sewing machine needle and have the type and size that is best suited for the kind of sewing you will be doing and the thread size and type you are using. See Volume 2, Class 210, Lesson Two (page 12–14).

❋ Always test dark, rich colors for colorfastness. See Volume 2, Class 220, Lesson Two (pages 17–20).

THE NEXT STEP

We are now entering into the exciting world of triangles. We extensively covered the use of squares and rectangles in Volumes 1 and 2, and now it is time to jazz things up a bit. Next to squares, triangles are the most commonly used shape in patchwork designs. There are many different ways to construct triangles, and we are going to take you through eight different methods of making half-square triangle units in Classes 310 and 320. Within some of these lessons you will find some optional ways of doing the same thing. The lessons in Class 310 will focus on methods that make single units at a time. These methods are great if you only need a few for a block or two, or if you are working with a very scrappy look in your quilt and don't want many repeats of the same fabric combinations showing up. The lessons in Class 320 will deal with making multiples of the same two fabrics. These methods make quick work of making enough half-square triangles for borders, sashing, multiples of the same block design, and so on.

Our goal here is to have you make sixteen half-square triangle units from each of the eight techniques presented. This is a good number to really get the idea of how the technique works. We strongly recommend that you work through each of the techniques and make the sixteen units. Use an envelope that you have labeled with the title of the technique to store the half-square units. We suggest that you make notes of your own experiences when working through each of the methods. Some of the methods give you a bit of fudge room to trim to the exact size once the sewing is done. Some of them finish at the size needed with no fudge room. This is the time for you to discover if your seam allowance is working for you or against you and ask yourself some questions: Are your units too small once the sewing and pressing is finished? Are the units square, and do you have corners where the seams are exactly in the corner? Does any single process seem like much more work compared with others? Take notes of what problems you encounter and your reaction to the result of each process.

Once you have worked through all of the techniques, Carrie will walk you through the basics of how to construct the sampler blocks using all the units from each technique to make the sampler table runner in Class 320 (page 28) or the quilt in Class 330 (page 40). This is a very important project, as you will experience working with seams that are pressed open as well as closed. You will learn how to avoid the pitfalls of points not aligning and will learn tips on how to make the process as painless as possible.

note **IMPORTANT:** *It is critical that you construct the blocks for the sampler table runner, whether you make the table runner or not. The detailed hints for success will not be repeated in each of the projects that follow. This is where you really learn the ins and outs of precise piecing of half-square triangles.*

Once you complete the sampler blocks, you can choose any technique of your liking to make the *Broken Dishes* quilt top that follows the sampler blocks instructions. Your choice of technique will determine the amount of fabric you need to get through all the methods. By looking closely at the *Broken Dishes* quilt as well as the sampler blocks, decide what fabrics you want to work with—planned or scrappy.

BASIC START-UP HINTS

Before we get started, we want to help you be as successful as possible by sharing a few basic hints for sewing bias edges and working with rulers.

SLOW DOWN

First, it is important that you slow down your sewing when working with bias. We are sure you found that when sewing strips and then chaining squares together, you could speed up and sew fairly quickly. That is not the case with these techniques. Bias is very stretchy and can easily be distorted when you are sewing too fast. Triangles are time-consuming, but ripping is even more so, so slow down and enjoy the process and the precision.

ACCURATE POINTS

When you are sewing the points at the beginning and end of each bias seam, the points have a tendency to veer off to one side or the other, which causes them to waver. We will address trimming these points off in the lessons later. When this happens, it is next to impossible for the triangle units to be square and accurate. Start by sewing a scrap of fabric and having it under the foot when you sew the first unit. We discussed this in Volume 1, Class 130 (page 25). The scrap keeps the thread from getting jammed and gives you a clean start on the triangle unit. Start with your needle down just beyond the edge of the scrap. As you position the diagonal seam, lift the presser foot up and slide the point under the foot. You might find using a stiletto helpful for positioning the fabric under the foot.

Placing point up against the edge of the needle using a stiletto

If you don't have total mastery of your foot control, start sewing by lowering the presser foot and manually taking a couple of stitches using the flywheel of the machine with your right hand and guiding the fabric with your left. Be sure that you turn the flywheel toward you, never backward. If the foot control starts too quickly, the sudden speed can easily cause you to lose control of the bias edge and/or jam the thread in the bobbin area of your machine. Start the machine slowly and make sure that the raw edge of the seam is just gliding alongside your barrier seam guide. It is time well spent to consciously train your foot to regulate the foot control. See if you can take one stitch at a time by making quick, short presses on the foot control. If your foot control has a down-needle position built into it (we just rock our heel toward the floor to lower the needle on our machines), it is very useful to know how to control this—it leaves your hands at the needle at all times and your foot in control of the needle.

> *tip* If you are working on a Bernina and are using the #13 foot, you might want to add a thick piece of tape in front of the guide bar to give you even more guidance with the bias seams.

As you approach the upcoming end point, stop about 1″ away from the point. Place the index finger of your left hand just beside the left edge of the presser foot. Press down a bit. With your right hand, position your stiletto in about ¼″ from the point and use it to guide the point in under the foot. Sew slowly. By doing this, you will be able to keep the seam allowance tracking perfectly straight. If you are lucky enough to be using a straight-stitch foot with a narrow toe on the right and a guide bar, you can watch the edge of the fabric feed all the way under the foot by watching the inside edge of the guide bar the entire distance of the toes of the foot to the needle. This will assist in sewing very straight seams right up to the points.

Finger and stiletto placement

Stop the needle just at the edge of the triangle. To position the next pair of triangles to be sewn, raise the presser foot, place the raw edge of the seam up against the barrier guide, and overlap the points until the needle is just at the raw edge of the next pair. (If your machine has a presser-foot knee-lift system, this is a perfect place to put it to use.) There will be only one stitch between the two sets of triangles. Once you have all the pairs sewn, end with another scrap.

Positioning second pair of triangles

> *tip* A straight-stitch throat plate is a valuable tool when sewing triangles, as the needle is not able to push fabric down into the hole of the throat plate, which can cause the fabric to shift when you come to the end of any seam. If the bed of your machine has any uneven areas, or the sewing table does not fit tightly and evenly, the use of a SewSlip II (by Gossamer Designs LLC) can also be a real help. There is a cutout that accommodates the feed dogs, and the Teflon sheet sticks to the bed of the machine and sewing area. This creates a consistent and even working surface for the fabric to slide on.

SewSlip II and straight-stitch throat plate

RULER CONTROL

When cutting squares and triangles, as well as when squaring triangle units, control of the ruler is very important. If you fight ruler slippage, try using something to stabilize your ruler. Invisi-Grip is a pressure-sensitive plastic by Omnigrid that is cut a bit smaller than your ruler and smoothed onto the back of the ruler. You can see through it, but it helps the ruler stick to the fabric.

Fabric Grips (by Collins)—little self-stick sandpaper dots—placed on the back of your ruler will also help prevent slippage. Place them where they will not interfere with your ability to read the lines of the ruler. They will wear down after a lot of use but can be peeled off and replaced.

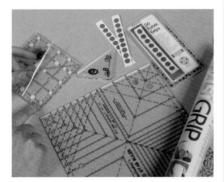

Invisi-Grip and Fabric Grips

When trimming a square made with two triangles, the most important thing to keep in alignment is the point of the ruler when it is in the corner of the sewn unit. The ruler line in the corner needs to be *exactly* aligned with the seam. While cutting, this corner is the most likely place for the ruler to slip. Place either the index or middle finger of the hand you are holding the ruler with right in the corner of the ruler and press down firmly. This stabilizes the corner and prevents the cutter from pushing the ruler out of position.

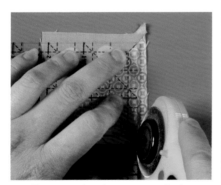

Finger pressing down corner of ruler

PRESSING

Pressing triangle units can be a bit tricky. Many of you may find that you are a bit heavy-handed with an iron, and steam gets you into big trouble. If this is the case, you might want to finger-press your triangle units into position before using an iron on them. By establishing the fold with your fingers, you have control of the points. Once you have a firm crease and the points are set, then pressing can be done with the iron.

LET'S START

You will be making sixteen units from each of the eight methods in Classes 310 and 320. All the methods make 2½″ unfinished units. Once the half-square triangles for each method are finished, place the sixteen units in separate envelopes or plastic bags until all the techniques are finished. Mark the envelopes with the technique used. You will use all of the units from each technique at the end to construct the sampler blocks. You might find it useful to take notes as you work through each technique. This is helpful to remind yourself of your likes and dislikes, your successes and problems, and solutions you work out to any problems you encounter for each method.

Before you start each technique, we need to address the way half-square triangle units are handled in most books and patterns. It is assumed that you can cut, sew, press, and end up with a half-square triangle unit that is perfectly square, in which the seam is exactly in the corners of the square, and that each unit is exactly the size needed with no problems. This

seldom happens for a beginner, and the result is corners that are missing or offset when piecing the units together. The object of these lessons is for you to try several common techniques and find out what works for you. After you have experienced them all, you can understand why different methods are valuable for different projects and why so many quilters prefer so many different techniques. There is not any one correct way or best technique; it is totally a personal preference.

> *tip* Whenever you sew on a bias edge, it is very important to starch the fabric before cutting it to help prevent it from stretching when you are sewing and pressing it. Use spray *starch*, not sizing. We are not talking stiff, but the fabric should have a crisp feel.

EXERCISE: MAKING MATHEMATICALLY CORRECT TRIANGLES

To cut a half-square triangle and get straight grain on the two short sides of the triangle, take the size of the finished triangle, in this case 2″, and add ⅞″ for seam allowance (2 + ⅞ = 2⅞). Cut a strip of light and a strip of dark fabric 2⅞″ wide. Cut these strips into a few 2⅞″ squares. The diagram below shows where this measurement comes from.

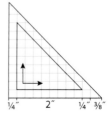

Seam allowances needed for triangle

Cut these squares in half diagonally corner-to-corner, creating 2 triangles for each square. Place 1 dark and 1 light triangle right sides together. (The strips can be cut right sides together, automatically placing the triangles in position for sewing. A little starch when pressing will help the 2 strips stick together.) Carefully sew the diagonal edge, using your seam guide, stiletto, and fingers to keep the pieces straight and accurate. Remember that you are sewing a bias edge, which can stretch very easily. Sew slowly. Don't forget to use your finger and stiletto to help guide the last ½″ through the foot, as discussed earlier (page 9).

You can chainstitch the triangle pieces one after another. Once sewn, press the seam allowance to the dark side.

Measure your finished units to see if they are exactly 2½″ square. If they are too small, your seam allowance was too wide. If they are a little large, the seam allowance was too narrow. The main benefit to cutting exact measurements is that the finished unit should be exact and ready for the next step. If this didn't happen, you might find the techniques in some of the following lessons that use mathematically correct measurements or specialized rulers will help make this process more accurate. In the other methods covered, you will cut the units larger and trim after pressing, resulting in a more foolproof finished product.

Yardage needed for Lessons Three through Six in Class 310 and Lessons Two through Five in Class 320:

❋ **Two-color combination (square sampler in Class 330, page 40):**

1 yard light for background

1 yard medium or dark for triangles

❋ **Three-color combination (table runner):**

1 yard background

½ yard or 1 fat quarter*, each medium or dark for triangles

(Fabric choices can be various prints of the same color and similar value. If you are making either style of the sampler, mixing the fabrics up can create more interest. If this is what you decide on, use the yardage for the scrappy quilt— just work in one color family.)

*Remember to check if your quilt shop is cutting or tearing their fat quarters—if they are cutting them, you will be better off just buying yardage so you can tear the fabric yourself to get it back on grain. (For a refresher on this see Volume 2, Class 220, page 20.)

Carrie's Note

There is a method to the madness with the block and color selection / combination in the Christmas Table Runner. The four blocks on the ends of the runner have their seam allowances pressed to one side, while those in the center (the red blocks) all have their seam allowances pressed open. I will explain this more when you reach the block construction instructions, but in the meantime, here is a list by technique number as to which color fabric you will be working with and how you will be pressing your seam allowance:

Green fabric with seam allowances pressed toward the green—Techniques 1, 2, 7, and 8.

Red fabric with seam allowances pressed open—Techniques 3, 4, 5, and 6.

LESSON THREE:
Rotary-cut triangles— Method #1

When making stacks of half-square triangles for a quilt, the last thing you want to encounter is several of the units not being square or large enough to use. We prefer to cut the strips larger than mathematically correct so that once the units are sewn, they can be cut down to size for a perfect half-square triangle. This method allows you to rotary cut individual triangles without using any kind of template or guide.

If you are making the table runner, you will want to use the fabric you have planned for the blocks that have the green fabric in them.

Begin by straightening your fabric, ironing both the light and dark fabrics right sides together. Starch and remove all folds. Fold in half just once and cut your strips. If you are using fat quarters, you will have a piece 18″ × 11″ approximately; if using a ⅓- or ½-yard piece, you will have a 12″ or 18″ × 22″ piece. This lets you cut both strips at the same time, ensuring that the edges align exactly. You will add 1″ instead of ⅞″ to the finished size of the triangle. In this case, you will cut the strips 3″ wide (2 + 1 = 3″). You need 2 strips 3″ wide if you are using fat quarters, as you will get 7 squares from 1 strip and will only need a single square from the second. Set the remainder of the second strip aside to use for a later technique. You will only need a single strip of the 2 fabrics, pressed together, if you are using yardage. Again, set the leftovers aside to be used later.

Once the strips are cut, square off the end of the strips and then measure down the length of the strip and cut 8 – 3″ squares. Cut these squares in half diagonally. Once you align the ruler exactly in the corners, angle your cutter blade a bit so that you are not adding the width of the blade to the side of the ruler. If you don't do this, one side of triangles will be slightly larger than the other. You can also offset the ruler by a thread and cut with the cutter straight.

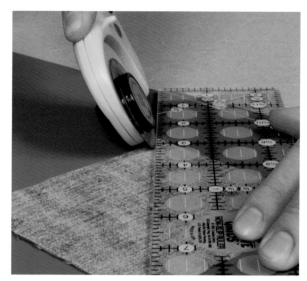

Cutting squares in half

Carrie's Hint

You may find that as you cut away from yourself, the square under the ruler shifts a little, making the cut off-center. To compensate, you can cut halfway through the square from the corner closest to you to the center of the square and then stop and cut from the other corner down toward the center, pulling the rotary cutter toward you, keeping everything aligned with the ruler. Remember to keep a finger in each corner of the ruler to prevent slippage.

As you cut the squares into triangles, alternate them in a stack so that they are easy to pick up and feed into the machine. Because you layered the fabric right sides together before cutting, the triangles are ready to sew once cut. This eliminates needing to realign the edges of separate pieces.

Alternating triangles in stack

Chainstitch the triangle pieces one after another, sewing on the long side of the triangle. Be sure to follow the instructions under Accurate Points (page 8) before starting to sew these together.

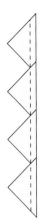

Chainstitch and clip apart.

Clip the units apart and press the seam allowance toward the darker side. When pressing, be sure you don't pull on the triangle you are pressing toward with your hand, as this will stretch the bias, and the triangle unit will get out of square. Set the seam closed first, and then use the weight of the iron and the point to gently push the triangle over the seam allowance. Be especially careful at the corners, making sure there is not a pleat pressed in the seam on the front side. Make sure the seam is straight to the very tip. Once the half-square unit is open, lightly spray it with starch and push the front edge of the iron up against the seam to flatten and set it. Do not get aggressive with these pieces. Once they are out of square, it is next to impossible to get them to have accurate points when piecing the units together.

Pressing with side of iron

Once the units are pressed, you will need to trim the triangle squares to size. You will achieve perfect points by taking the time to trim exactly. The Precision Trimmer 6 by Marsha McCloskey is our preferred ruler for trimming half-square triangle units. It has diagonal lines as well as the cut measurement lines to square up with so you know you are cutting exactly. You can use any square ruler of your choice, but you might find that all the busyness of the multiple lines makes it hard to align your unit and stay accurate for trimming.

Align the diagonal ruler line on your seamline. Split the difference in the extra that needs to be trimmed off on all 4 sides. Make sure that the actual corner of the ruler and the diagonal line printed on the ruler are *exactly* on the seam. It is helpful to place your finger as close to the edge of the ruler in the corner as you feel comfortable and press firmly. This will keep the ruler from slipping when you're running the cutter along the side of the ruler at the corner. It is also *extremely* helpful to have a new blade when trimming. A dull blade puts drag on the cutter and can cause ruler slippage and miscut edges.

Cut both sides of the corner. Turn the half-square triangle unit around 180° and realign, making sure the seam is exactly on the diagonal line and the corner of the ruler is aligned exactly with the seam. Cut the remaining 2 sides. You now have a perfect 2½″ half-square triangle unit. Repeat this trimming process for the remaining 15 units and lay them aside.

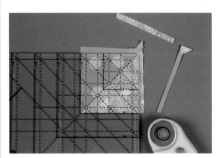

Trimming with Precision Trimmer 6

tip As you trim the squares to size, be sure to check each one to make sure that the seam runs exactly to the cut corner. If the seam is even a thread off the corner, it will be difficult to get sharp, accurate points when you begin to piece the squares together.

Seam exactly at corner

JUDY MARTIN'S POINT TRIMMER

What if you really dislike the trimming needed when adding 1″ to the cutting measurement, and you can sew the mathematically correct pieces (⅞″) accurately? Here is a tool that you might want to consider.

You will notice that the triangles have long, skinny points. These "ears" need to be trimmed away, either before they are sewn or after they are pressed. We find that if you pre-trim the units before you sew, it eliminates the problem of the points not feeding under the foot correctly and gives you a blunt edge to push under the foot as you begin the seam. These trimmed corners also help you align your patches perfectly when piecing the blocks together. A very handy tool is Judy Martin's Point Trimmer. This little tool will help you trim the seam allowance points for more accurate piecing.

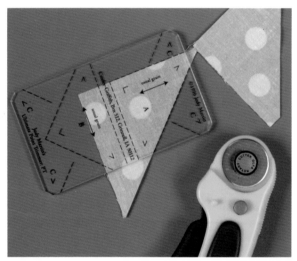

Judy Martin's Point Trimmer

Once the pieces are sewn and pressed, the points are already trimmed and ready for the next step.

SCRAPMASTER

The ScrapMaster ruler is not a technique but a very handy ruler for cutting scraps into usable pieces. If you find you are starting to have a collection of leftover pieces that are too big to throw away and too small to put back on the shelf, you might want to consider cutting them into triangles or squares right then and there and storing these shapes for future use. We all know that digging through a tub of scraps, pressing them, and then cutting them is something we are unlikely to do very often. If the pieces are precut, they are ready for that scrap quilt anytime you need them.

Identify the grainline of the scrap. You want to make sure that the square corner of the triangle is on grain. Place the ruler over the fabric, keeping the square corner straight with the grain, and see what size you can get from the scrap. Cut the diagonal first.

Rotate the ruler and align the diagonal line with the edge you just cut at the size line that fits the scrap. Cut both sides of the corner.

Start a box for each of the different sizes you salvage from your scraps. These are free quilts when you get enough gathered up—and no cutting to get started!

 tip You can also use the Perfect Patchwork Templates for the same purpose as long as you have all the sizes you need.

LESSON FOUR:
Sew and slice—Method #2

This method is based on the same principles as Lesson Three, except you won't be precutting the squares into triangles. You will be sewing oversized squares, which are then cut apart, pressed, and trimmed to size. This eliminates sewing a cut bias edge.

Start by cutting 8 squares each of your chosen fabrics 1″ larger than the finished size of the desired triangle square. We are working with 2″ finished units, so cut your squares 3″. You can use the remainder of your leftover strips from Method #1, but you'll need to cut a second 3″-wide strip. Keeping both fabrics right sides together, cut the strips into 3″ squares.

Place a ruler point to point diagonally on the square, allowing just a thread off the corner to allow for the pencil line. Using a mechanical pencil, draw a line from corner to corner on the lighter fabric. Start drawing the line from the center of the square and draw to one corner. Be sure to stabilize the corner of the ruler as you draw the line. Repeat in the other direction. By starting in the center, the potential for the fabric to stretch is reduced. Keep the pencil angled away from the ruler when drawing the line. If the pencil is straight up and down, the width of the side of the pencil can easily be added. Have just the lead point up against the ruler.

DRAWING STITCHING LINES

If you don't have an accurate ¼" presser foot, you can draw another line ¼" away from the centerline on both sides, as sewing guidelines. The Perkins Dry Goods' Perfect Piecing Seam Guide can be used as a ruler by placing the scant ¼" line on top of the drawn centerline and then drawing another line as a stitching line. Do this on both sides of the centerline.

> *note* *When working with a ¼" piecing foot, you need to know if the foot is ¼" from the needle to the outside edge of the foot. (Measure this to be sure your foot is accurate.) If you allow the line to run beside the edge of the foot, you will be taking too wide a seam. To get a scant ¼" seam allowance, be sure that the line is just under the edge of the foot—the foot covering the line. This will be one thread narrower than the outside of the foot and will give you a scant ¼" seam. It is easier to keep your eye on the needle and guide it right inside the line than to try to guide off of a thick foot. You will need to do a sample or two to determine just how far from the line you need to be on your machine to get the accuracy you need. Thread weight and needle size also play a part in this. If your thread is heavy or your needle is large, you are apt to take too deep of a seam, which will make you sew farther from the line to compensate. Make samples until you get the right combination of needle, thread, and distance.*

The Quick Quarter, by Quilter's Rule, is another handy tool that has slots down the center to align with the points of the square. The sides are ¼" from the slots, so draw a line along both sides of the Quick Quarter to mark the seamlines.

Using Quick Quarter or Perkins' seam guide to draw stitching lines

THE ANGLER 2

Another handy tool is The Angler 2 (by Pam Bono Designs). This tool eliminates the need to draw lines on the squares at all. You cut the squares and use the guidelines on the angler to guide the fabric through the machine.

Follow the instructions carefully, as you have to get the angler attached to the bed of your machine straight and square before you can use it. If your machine does not have a flat sewing surface around the needle area, this product will not work for you. You need at least 3"–4" in front of and to the sides of your needle in order to tape the piece of plastic into position. If you are sewing large squares (larger than 7¾"), you will need to extend the lines beyond the plastic. Place a piece of painter's tape (we prefer this to masking tape, as it leaves no sticky residue) in front of the angler so you can extend the lines onto the tape. Using a straightedge, extend the three lines toward you. Now larger squares can be easily guided.

The Angler 2 in position with lines on tape to extend guidelines

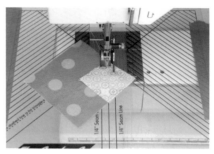

Position of square when using lines to guide

Beginning on the left side of the center diagonal line, stitch a scant ¼" alongside the drawn line.

If you are sewing one square at a time, lift the foot at the end of the square and turn the square around. Pull out about ½" of thread without clipping it. Now stitch the unsewn side of the line. If you are sewing multiples, chain sew one side of all the pairs, turn the chain around, and chain sew the second side.

OFFSETTING SEAMS

When chain sewing squares that have the stitching lines drawn on them, you can offset the seams for easier feeding under the foot. Start by positioning your needle one thread inside the left-side line (into the seam allowance allotment). Keep your needle running just beside this line the length of the seam. Once you get to the end of the line, position another square under the foot, this time aligning the needle with the inside of the right-side line. This lets the edges of the square snug up to one another and eliminates a lot of stitches between the pieces and overlapping corners. Once all the units are sewn on the first side, clip off the first one at the beginning of the chain and bring it to the front. Turn it so you can align the unsewn side with the needle and sew next to the line. Continue clipping one off and adding it to the chain until all the squares are stitched on both sides of the centerline.

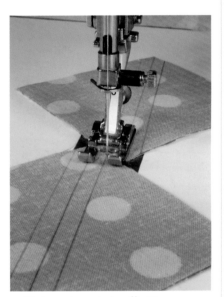

Chain sewing pairs by offsetting seams

Press the units flat before cutting to set the seam. Cut on the center diagonal line. Press the seams gently toward the darker fabric and starch. Using the Precision Trimmer 6, line up the diagonal line with the seam and trim the top and right side of the square. Turn the square 180° and realign the diagonal line and the 2½″ lines of the trimmer with the square. Trim the remaining 2 sides. You will have a perfect 2½″ triangle square. This method is foolproof!

hint When trimming, you might find it helpful to have a mat that rotates or a small mat that you can turn easily so that you don't have to move the pieces to line them up for trimming the other sides.

Rotating mats and small mat

tip You might find that the extra thickness at the corner of half-square triangle units can cause a bit of distortion when you're trimming. It is helpful to start at the corner each time you trim a side. Press straight down with the blade right at the corner, roll back off the ruler edge, and then roll the cutter down the ruler edge. If you push the cutter toward the corner, the fabric can easily shift a bit, and you will lose your point. Don't forget to press down with your finger on the corner of the ruler, and don't forget that a sharp blade is one of the most important parts of clean, accurate cutting.

Cutting from corner

Perfect Patchwork Templates— Method #3

Perfect Patchwork Templates come in sets of several different sizes and shapes. For our 2″ finished triangles, you will need Set B. The Corner Trimmer from Marti Michell is also available if you would rather rotary cut the triangles and then cut the corners. Cutting around the template is the most accurate, but it does take time and care to cut around the small shapes. You may find it very helpful to put sandpaper dots in the points and/or corners on the bottom of each template shape. This prevents the templates from sliding when you're cutting. Using a 28mm rotary cutter is highly recommended when you cut around templates. The smaller size of the blade allows for more flexibility and control when cutting small shapes. If you have a small rotary cutting mat (12″ × 18″ or smaller), it might be helpful to turn the mat instead of the fabric and template to make it easier and more accurate to cut around all the sides. Refer to the Hint about rotating mats.

Again, prepare your fabric by layering the 2 pieces right sides together; starch and press dry. Cut a strip 2½″ × 45″. Lay the layered strip on your cutting mat. Position the template (#13) so that one short side of the template is against the cut edge of the strip and the blunt end of the corner is on the opposite side of the strip. You will see that the suggested direction of the grain is marked on the template. Cut both sides of the template and then cut the corners. Rotate the template 180°, realign with the cut edges of the strips, and cut. Cut 16 sets.

Cutting with templates

If you find it tedious and awkward to cut around the template, you can cut strips, then squares, then triangles with your ruler. Use the template to confirm their accurate size, trim up the pieces if they are not accurate, and trim the corners.

note If you find you like the way these corners fit together when you start piecing the blocks, you will no doubt want them on all the points you piece. The Corner Trimmer is a triangle template that you can use on any size triangle or 45° angle to trim the double blunt points.

The blunt corners make for smooth chain piecing. Before you sew all 16 sets together, we suggest that you cut and sew a sample. If your seam allowance is different from what is built into the template, your triangles will not finish at the correct size. There is no marking on the templates to give you a guide for the seam allowance. We find that a scant ¼″ works best, but again, the size of your thread and your seam guide system will also need to be considered. Correct your seam guide if necessary before chain sewing the units for the sampler. Be aware that the cut of the point has nothing to do with the alignment of the seam but creates a perfect blunt corner when the pieces are pressed, so don't use the cut as a guide for setting your seam allowance for this method.

Once all 16 sets are stitched, press the seams open.

Carrie's Note
Just because you have cut around a template to create your perfect half-square triangle and have adjusted your seam allowance does not mean your squares will be exactly 2½″. So even if it seems tedious, make sure you double-check all your pieces using the Precision Trimmer 6 and trim away any extra threads. If you found being a few threads off to be frustrating when you were working with squares and rectangles, I can promise you that you will end up extremely annoyed by being a few threads off with triangles—take your time and double-check and trim everything!

tip You can use different templates within a set to square, true, or check the size of two or more triangles sewn together. If you have sewn two triangles together to make a square, use the square template to check for size and squareness. If you have sewn two triangles onto two sides of a square, use the larger triangle template the size of the three units sewn together to check for accuracy. This is also a good way to double-check that the corners have been sewn and trimmed exactly like the templates. These corners are the secret of the templates.

LESSON SIX:
Easy Angle— Method #4

Here is another technique that requires you to sew very accurately. The triangle units come out the exact size needed, with no fudge room for trimming.

tip If you find through doing all of these different methods that you like one that is cut to size, but you have trouble with accuracy, you can always cut the next size up. Stitch, press, and then trim the same way you would if you were using a method that starts with a larger unit.

To use this tool, cut strips of each fabric used in the triangle-square unit ½″ wider than the *finished* square desired. For example, if you're making 2″ triangle-square units, cut the strips 2½″ wide.

Place one of each of the different fabric strips right sides together, being very careful to keep the long edges even, or layer the 2 fabrics and cut the strips together at one time. Lay the strips on your cutting mat. Position the Easy Angle on the left end of the strip, keeping the black tip off the bottom edge. The number that corresponds with the width of the fabric strip appears at the top. The black tip on one point of the ruler will always be off the edge of the strip. In this example, the fabric strips are being cut 2½″, so the Easy Angle number will be 2½. Once the ruler is aligned properly, cut the angle with a rotary cutter. Remember to keep your finger at the top of the ruler to stabilize the point each time you make a cut.

First cut with Easy Angle

For the next cut, rotate the Easy Angle 180°. Line up the black tip so that it is off the top edge of the fabric strip. Cut on the right side. Return to the previous position to cut the next triangle. Continue down the length of the strip in this manner. Remember that the black tip is always off the edge of the fabric. You will need 16 sets.

Second cut

When sewing, you will find the blunt end very helpful for positioning one triangle up against the one before it. Again, because the ruler is allowing for the ⅞″ seam allowance allotment, you might want to sew one and press, then measure, to be sure your seam guide is set correctly for this method. Make the first couple of stitches manually to ensure a clean start.

Once all 16 are stitched, trim the long point at the end of each seam. You can do this before or after you have pressed. Press the seam open, lightly starch, and press dry. Using the Precision Trimmer 6, align the raw edges with the 2½″ lines and check for accuracy. If all went well, the units will not require any trimming and will be an accurate square. Check each of the corners at the seam to be sure that the seam is exactly in the corner.

LESSON SEVEN:
The blocks for the sampler
THE SAMPLER BLOCKS

Each of these blocks presents a different piecing strategy. Some work better with the seam pressed open, and others prefer the seam to one side. We will be walking you through each block to help you get precise points and well-nested seams. You will need to make an extra set of sixteen half-square triangle units for the ninth block if you choose to make the square quilt rather than the table runner. Use your favorite method for this extra block.

Fourteen blocks are illustrated here. You need to pick four that have what looks like a solid square in the center and four with a pinwheel in the center if you are making the table runner. If you chose to do the square quilt in Class 330, pick your favorite nine blocks!

Pinwheel

Our Editor

Mosaic

Whirlwind

Return of the Swallows Variation

Anna's Choice

Star of the Milky Way

Colorado Block

Colorado Quilt Variation

Magic Cross

Peace and Plenty

Yankee Puzzle

Barbara Frietchie Star

Hourglass

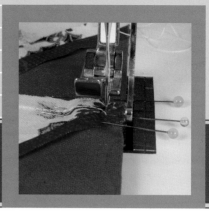

Class 320

Workspace ideas

In the previous two volumes of this series, we gave you a number of ideas for using a small space to make a sewing area, storage ideas for your fabric, and formulas for how to figure how much lighting you need in your room if you have a dedicated sewing room. Now we would like to list some of the pitfalls to avoid and issues to consider when you set up your sewing area, whether in a dedicated room or on the dining room table.

The first thing to consider is your electrical needs and where that power has to come from. As we talked about in Volume 2, Class 240 (page 35), if you are sewing in a bedroom or your basement, it is likely that the outlets in those rooms share a circuit with at least one other room in your house. The number of outlets you have may be limited. In either of these cases, it is a good idea to invest in a high-quality surge protector power bar. Make sure to choose one that isn't just for expanding the number of plug-ins you have, but one that has a trip switch in it that will flip when a large amount of power is being used from that one source. It will shut off the power to the items plugged into

it, rather than allowing the breaker in your electrical panel to be tripped. Spending $30–$50 on a good surge protector is far cheaper than having to have an electrician come out to replace your breaker or add a circuit.

If you can't afford an electrician to come out and upgrade your lighting, make the most of what light you do have. Carrie has been discovering that as she expands her sewing area in her basement, light and shadows are a problem. Here are some of the issues Carrie has encountered for you to consider. In her basement, she has a ceiling fan and two other small fixtures in the ceiling that provide all of the overhead light she has to work with. The ceiling fan has three 60-watt bulbs, and the other two fixtures have two 75-watt bulbs. She also only has two wall outlets in the room, and they are about fifteen feet from one another. The challenge has been to make an efficient work area that makes the best use of the light and power available. To start, she measured and graphed out her room on graph paper and then measured her various furniture pieces, drew them to scale, and cut them out of graph paper. On her room diagram she made notes of the windows, light fixtures, and outlets, and then started to

play with her furniture. This is something you can do too. Graph paper is not only useful for designing quilts!

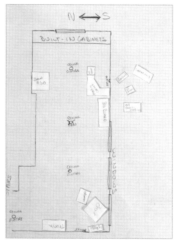

Graph paper diagram of sewing room with outlets, lighting, and windows indicated

The solution Carrie has come up with is to increase the number of task lights she has around her sewing machine so that she can use the overhead lighting to its best advantage over the ironing board. She found that overall light is much more important at the ironing board than it is at the sewing machine. She also found it easy to supplement her light at the sewing machine with two Daylight lamps (by Daylight Company) to illuminate the area around her needle. This allowed her to sew in a rather shadowed area of the room, so she could keep her ironing board close by her sewing area but have the ironing board area lit as well as possible. Because her ironing board is also her cutting table, she moved a task light onto the ironing board right next to her cutting mat when she was trimming or cutting fabric.

While this is not an ideal situation, it works well for now. When she can fit it into the budget, she plans to put in large overhead fluorescent light fixtures that will eliminate the shadowing issue. In the meantime, being focused on how to best use what she has is working well.

The same thought process is true for your fabric storage. Streamlining how and where you store things based on how you work in your space will always serve you best. You can pick up some great ideas from organization books, but it all comes down to how you use your space and what makes sense to you. Take your time in setting up your sewing area and know that things will change depending on what aspect of quilting you are focusing on—the piecing or the actual quilting of the tops you are making.

Just as another idea, we have a customer at the store who is finally getting to move her sewing area into a room by itself. She has been thinking about this move for over a year and has been very conscious of how she works in her space. She is going to convert the entire closet to her storage area, with shelves to put her fabric on. She has a big board that she is going to mount on top of two stock base kitchen cabinets that will give her extra storage. She has another two base cabinets that her husband is going to put a countertop on for her cutting area. She is then planning a supplemental ironing board area

(a wall-mounted folding ironing board) that she will place to the left of her sewing machine so that she can use the board not only for pressing seams quickly when piecing but also as extra support for her quilts as she quilts them. All of this is fitting into an eight-by-ten-foot room—talk about an efficient use of space.

If you haven't developed a design wall yet, here is a quick and inexpensive way to solve the problem—purchase a flannel-backed vinyl tablecloth. They are heavy and durable, and the flannel on the backside is fairly fuzzy. Place it in a low-temperature dryer to take out the fold lines and wrinkles and staple or tack it to a wall. This will be a great help as you are designing increasingly complex quilts that you need to see develop before sewing them.

LESSON TWO:
Sheeting triangles— Method #5

One of the first speed techniques for making half-square triangles was developed simultaneously by Barbara Johanna and Ernest Haight. They independently developed the method in the early 1970s. This method is commonly referred to as "sheeting up," and it requires that you draw the units on the fabric before sewing. A more modern version of this technique—which we will use in Lesson Five—uses paper foundations.

Sheeting is one of the fastest methods for producing many units of the same fabric combination. It is not the best for scrap quilts, where a variety of fabrics are needed for the triangle squares. Fat quarters are the best size to work with for quantity, but any size fabric

piece will work. You will be working with a 10″ square to make the 16 triangle squares needed for this lesson.

Start by placing 1 piece of each fabric, right sides together, with the light fabric on top, and press. Starch lightly and press dry. This helps the fabrics to stick together. You will be drawing a grid directly onto the light fabric.

You again have a choice as to what method of math you want to use. If you find that you are accurate when sewing against a line and your pieces are coming out the right size, you can draw the grid using the finished size of the unit needed plus ⅞″. If you prefer to trim and make sure every corner is dead-on, add 1″ to the finished size of the triangle square you need. For every square you draw, you will get 2 finished triangle-square units.

Using a long ruler, draw a line parallel to and ½″ from the selvage along the entire length of the fabric. Continue to draw parallel lines, each 2⅞″ (or 3″ for trimming) apart, across the fabric.

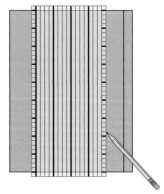

Drawing parallel lines to selvage

Now you're ready to draw the cross lines. Using the horizontal lines on the ruler, line them up exactly with the lines on the fabric. If you are using the ⅞″ seam allowance method, take extra care in drawing the squares, as there is no fudge room if the lines are off a bit. The first line will be about ½" from one edge. Continue drawing lines 2⅞" (or 3") apart, intersecting with the previously drawn lines perfectly, until you're to the edge of the fabric.

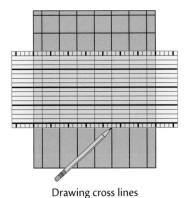

Drawing cross lines

Next, draw diagonal lines in every other square, starting in one corner.

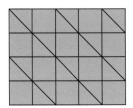

Drawing first set of diagonal lines

Draw diagonal lines in the opposite direction in the remaining empty squares. Once all the lines are drawn, pin in every blank space.

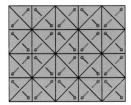

Drawing second set of diagonal lines

Using your favorite foot and/or method for sewing next to a line, begin the stitching as illustrated below. Stitch in a continuous line, using the same side of your presser foot consistently. You will be sewing beyond lines on the edge and turning corners. Continue sewing until all the diagonal lines have stitching on both sides.

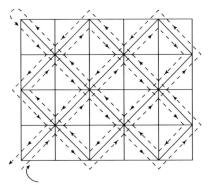

Stitching in direction of arrows

> **tip** The continuous sewing process works for any size piece of fabric as long as one side is an odd number of grid squares.

Using your rotary cutter and ruler, begin separating the rows by cutting on all the straight lines of one direction.

> **tip** The most efficient way to cut these squares apart is to not let them separate as you move the ruler. Position the ruler for the first cut. Once the cutting is completed, place the fingers of one hand at the end of the ruler. Gently tip the other end up with your other hand. If you do this carefully and slowly, the fabric will not be disturbed as it would be if you slide the ruler.

Tipping ruler up with hand

Continue by carefully aligning the ruler with the cut edges and cut on the remaining straight lines to cut the rows into squares.

The last cuts are the diagonals. If you have been very careful in moving your ruler, the sheet of fabric will still be aligned before you cut. Carefully place the ruler on the diagonal lines and cut. If the fabric has moved out of alignment, cut the squares in half diagonally, one by one.

Once all the squares are cut in half diagonally, press the seam to the dark triangle, starch lightly, and trim if necessary.

For the exercise in this method, you will cut 2 – 10" squares of your fabric. Follow the instructions above to draw the grid on the fabric. You will have a grid that is 3 × 3, using either the 2⅞" or the 3" measurement. When you start to sew, you will find that you need to stop and start 3 times. First, stitch on the diagonal line that goes corner to corner. The next line makes a rectangle in the center of the square. Stitch the inside of the rectangle first, and then move to the other side of the line and go around the rectangle again. Once the sewing is done, press, starch lightly, and cut the units apart. You will have 18 half-square triangle units.

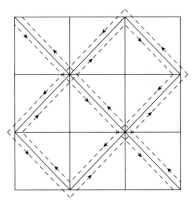

Stitching direction lines

LESSON THREE:

Bias strips— Method #6

The original bias strip technique was shared with Marsha McCloskey by one of her students many years ago, and Marsha and Nancy Martin have made it a staple technique in many books from That Patchwork Place (Martingale Publishing) over the past 20+ years. We will walk you through three different methods for working with bias strips. You can choose one of the methods for your sample blocks.

These methods are actually a form of strip piecing. Strips of fabric are cut on the bias and sewn together into a specific formation. The half-square triangle units are then cut from the bias strip set with a Bias Square ruler. The 45° line on the ruler is aligned with the seamline to make the cut. The resulting cut squares will have the straight grain along the outer edges.

Layer 2 fabrics with right sides together and cut a 12″ square. Use a large square rotary-cutting ruler to cut both squares at the same time. Once the square is cut, make one long cut diagonally corner to corner across the square. This starts the bias strips. Measure over 2½″ and cut again. Continue until the whole square has been cut into bias strips.

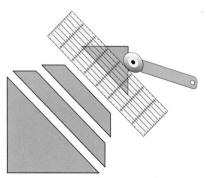

Cutting bias strips

note To determine the width of the bias strips to cut, on graph paper draw the finished size of the half-square triangle unit. Draw a diagonal line corner to corner through the square. Measure the distance from the center diagonal line to a corner of the square. Add ¾″ to this dimension for the needed strip width. If the number is not ruler friendly, round up to a number that can be easily cut using the markings on your ruler.

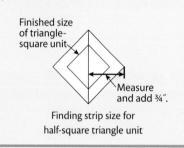

Finished size of triangle-square unit

Measure and add ¾″.

Finding strip size for half-square triangle unit

METHOD ONE

Sew the pairs of strips that are right sides together on one long bias edge. Press the seam open, especially for units that finish 1¾″ or smaller. We like to press the seams open for this technique to eliminate the ruler rocking over the seam when we're cutting the squares. Continue sewing all the pairs of strips of all lengths together and press. Sew the longest side of the longest pairs together, then the next longest, and so on. You will finish up with a piece that looks like the following illustration. Be sure to keep the points along the bottom edge even.

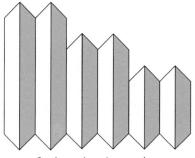

Sewing strip pairs together

Carrie's Note

A note about choosing how to press your seam allowances on half-square triangles. While you will find that there is much less distortion in the finished unit when you press your seams open, you will find that many blocks you make with these units need to have seams butted or nested together for accuracy. You can end up with a bit of a lump where all those layers of fabric intersect in your seam. You might experience this when you make the four green blocks for the table runner. If your seam allowance is pressed open, you have a much flatter, nicer seam area to deal with, but you have to use a pin to align your points. If you are planning to do any ditch quilting on the block, there is no ditch when the seams are pressed open. These are all things that you will need to think about as you make the eight (or nine) blocks for the sampler, and in the future when you make a quilt using many triangles.

Begin cutting at either end on the lower points of the strips. Align the 45° line of the Bias Square ruler on the seamline. Each bias square will need 2 cuts. Your first cut will be along the top and side edges of the ruler. This will separate the square from the set of strips. The second cut is made along the remaining 2 sides. Turn the square around, position the 45° line on the seam, and align the previously cut sides perfectly with the 2½″ measurement on the ruler. This will give you a perfect 2½″ cut half-square triangle unit.

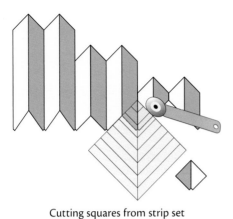

Cutting squares from strip set

> **tip** You can make all the first cuts and then trim the second side all at the same time. Watch for the notch that occurs when you cut each square from the strip set. Move the ruler up ¼″ on the seam to clear the notch before cutting each unit from the strip set.

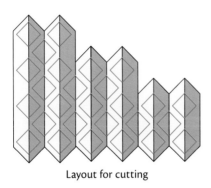

Layout for cutting

Continue cutting your half-square triangle units from each set of bias strips in the same manner, working from left to right, bottom to top, and row by row until you have cut your units from all the usable fabric. As you cut the outside strips, you will get "waste" triangles. These triangles are singles and can be trimmed to size with the ScrapMaster ruler and sewn together with other singles to get extra squares.

The following chart will help you determine what size square you need to cut your bias strips from to yield a given number of triangle squares.

Bias squares: Strips widths and square yields

Finished size	Cut size	Square size	Strip width	Yield (approx.)
1″	1½″ × 1½″	8″	2″	21
1″	1½″ × 1½″	12″	2″	50
1″	1½″ × 1½″	15″	2″	84
2″	2½″ × 2½″	10″	2½″	13
2″	2½″ × 2½″	12″	2½″	16
2″	2½″ × 2½″	15″	2½″	29
2½″	3″ × 3″	8″	2¾″	8
2½″	3″ × 3″	14″	2¾″	20
2½″	3″ × 3″	15″	2¾″	27
3″	3½″ × 3½″	9″	3¼″	8
3″	3½″ × 3½″	14″	3¼″	16
3″	3½″ × 3½″	15″	3¼″	19

> **tip** All three of the methods presented in this lesson are great for scrappy combinations. Cut a variety of fabrics into 6″–9″ squares and cut the squares into bias strips. Mix and match the strips before sewing them together for a wonderful variety of combinations. 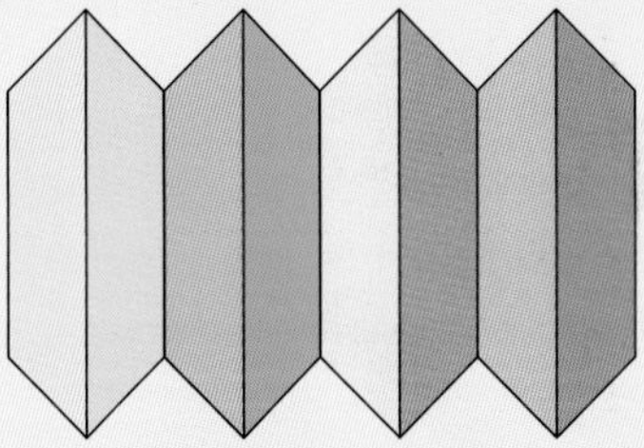
>
> Using a variety of fabrics

METHOD TWO

If you need a considerable number of triangle squares, you can work with fat quarters (18″ × 22″) or even fat eighths (9″ × 22″). The process is the same, but the strip set will look different when all the strips are sewn together, as you will have several strips of the same length to join.

Start by layering the 2 fabrics together, both right sides up. Make the first cut from one corner, making sure it is at a 45° angle to the edge. A large square ruler is helpful when making the first cut. Lay the square ruler on the edge, the 45° line aligned with the fabric edge. Lay a long ruler next to the square. This will establish the first cut. Proceed with cutting strips the size you need.

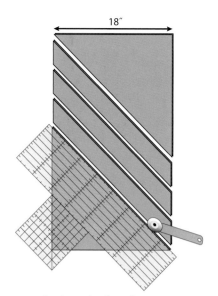

18″

Cutting strips from fat quarter

Arrange the strips in the order you are going to sew them. You will be laying out 2 sets of strips at once. Start with the small triangle in either corner. Each one is the beginning of a strip set. Take both of the next longer strips; lay the light one next to the dark small triangle and a dark one next to the light small triangle. Repeat this with each pair of strips until your layout matches the one in the illustration below.

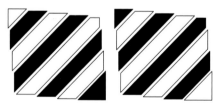

Strip set from fat quarter

When sewing the strips together, be sure to keep the lower edge and the left side in a straight line. This will enable you to get the highest yield from the strips.

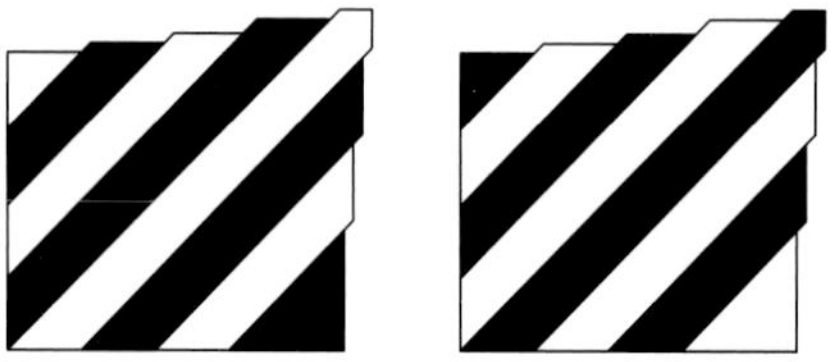

Strips set with lower and left edge straight

You will begin cutting at the left lower edge. Using a Bias Square ruler, align the 45° line on the seamline. You will need to make 2 cuts for each bias square. The first cut will be a square; the second cut will be a rectangle. Once all the squares are removed from the strip set, you can trim them to the correct size.

Cutting squares from square strip set

Fat quarter cutting chart for bias squares (based on 18″ × 22″ fat quarter)

Finished size	Cut size of bias square	Strip width	Yield
1″	1½″	1¾″	160
1¼″	1¾″	2″	120
1½″	2″	2″	100
1¾″	2¼″	2¼″	80
2″	2½″	2½″	60
2½″	3″	2¾″	50
3″	3½″	3¼″	38
4″	4½″	3¾″	24

METHOD THREE

Method Three still uses bias strips, but they are not going to be sewn together as we have done in the previous two methods. Instead, they will be paired up, right sides together, and sewn on both long sides of each pair. Quilter's Rule distributes a ruler designed by Alice Walter and her daughter Deb Hopkins. We discovered this ruler (Wonder Cut Ruler by Walter Times Two) in 2002, and

it makes quick work of dealing with bias strips. The math is built into the ruler—all you have to know is the unfinished size of the half-square triangle units you want. The instructions on the ruler have you cut straight-grain strips, but that leaves you with bias on all four edges of the finished units. Therefore, we are recommending you use bias strips so that all four edges are straight grain.

The ruler is marked with lines that indicate the *unfinished* size of your half-square triangles and the width you need to cut your strips. If you are working with large pieces of fabric to cut into bias strips, measure from the line for the unfinished size you need to the edge of the ruler that says "cut along this edge." Your 6″ × 24″ ruler can then be used to cut strips when the Wonder Cut Ruler is not long enough. We suggest that you lay the 2 pieces of fabric right sides together, starch and press, and cut both at the same time.

Cutting strips with Wonder Cut Ruler

Once the strips are cut, stitch along both long sides of each pair of strips using your seam allowance.

You will now turn the ruler and use the corner to cut the strips into triangles. Lay the line for the desired size of the *unfinished* half-square triangle along one long edge of the fabric. Cut along both edges of the ruler.

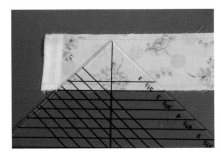

Cutting the first triangle

Next, turn over either the fabric strips or your ruler, align the ruler with the edge of the fabric again, and make one cut. Continue this process down the length of the fabric strip. If you are careful, these should come out to the exact size unit you need, without trimming.

Cutting second triangle

Press carefully and measure to check for accuracy. This method will help you make very scrappy combinations when you need them. You can sew any number of different combinations together to get different triangle units.

Wonder Cut Ruler yields per 42″-long strip

Size of triangle units	Yield
2″	27
2½″	22
3″	18
3½″	15
4″	13
4½″	12
5″	11
5½″	9

LESSON FOUR:

Eight from a square —Method #7

A fun and fast way to make eight half-square triangles at a time is to work with squares. Refer to the following chart to find the size squares to cut for the size half-square triangles you need.

Cutting sizes for eight from a square

Finished size	Cut squares	Trim to
1″	4″	1½″
1½″	5″	2″
2″	6″	2½″
2½″	7″	3″
3″	8″	3½″
3½″	9″	4″
4″	10″	4½″

Begin by placing both fabrics right sides together. Starch and press them together to help them stick to each other. On your cutting board, cut enough squares to yield the total number of units you need for your project. For this lesson, you will need 2 – 6″ squares of each fabric.

On the light square, draw diagonal lines with a mechanical pencil from corner to corner in both directions. Sew ¼″ on both sides of each line.

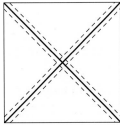

Drawing lines and sewing ¼″ from each side of each line

Press the squares and lightly starch again. Lay the squares on your cutting mat. You will need a 3½″-wide ruler to make the first cuts. Position the ruler 3″ from a straight side and cut the square side to side. Repeat for the other side. Be careful not to disturb the squares or allow the pieces to move after cutting.

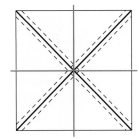

Cutting side to side both directions

Carefully place the ruler on one diagonal line and cut; then lifting the ruler gently, place it on the opposite line and cut. The reason for cutting the straight cuts first is if the pieces move, you still have a line to follow for the bias cuts.

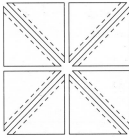

Cutting on the diagonal lines

You now have 8 half-square triangle units. They will be a bit oversized, so you will be trimming them to size once they are pressed. Press to the dark triangle, lightly starch, and press them dry. Trim them using the Precision Trimmer or a small square rotary ruler.

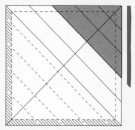

Alignment of Triangle Square Up Ruler

You really can't get much easier than this for making several half-square triangle units at a time.

LESSON FIVE:
Triangle paper— Method #8

Triangle paper has been available for quite some time. It comes in many varieties, but the original was Triangles on a Roll. Later came large sheets of newsprint printed with the grid called Half-Square Triangle Paper (no longer available). Now there are many versions; the most well known is Thangles. All of these products come in various sizes and eliminate the need to draw lines on the fabric. The grid and the guidelines for sewing are printed on the paper, which is pinned onto the fabric. We will be working with Triangles on a Roll (by HQS, Inc.). Just remember when you use these products to sew very carefully, as there is no allotment for trimming.

Determine how many units you need. Remember that each square yields 2 finished triangle-square units. Cut a length off the roll or a section from the sheet to accommodate the number needed. Layer 2 fabrics right sides together and press. Pin the paper on top through the fabric layers. Place the pins in the blank areas so you won't sew over them.

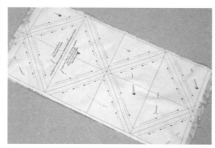

Triangle paper pinned to fabric

Use a setting of 15 stitches per inch (about 1.5) on your machine. This small stitch ensures that the paper is perforated when stitched. This makes removing the paper easier in the end. Because the paper is printed using the ⅞" seam allowance allotment, be sure to sew alongside the line on the seam allowance side to allow for the scant ¼" needed to make the half-square triangle units come out the right size. Stitch following the instructions for sheeted triangles, or the ones printed on the paper.

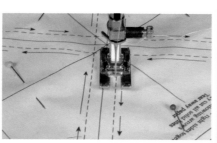

Sewing through the paper

Once the stitching is done, cut on the straight lines of the paper first and then on the diagonal lines.

Once all the triangles are cut and separated, fold the paper back against the stitching and make a sharp crease. This helps to release the paper. At the center of the seam, gently pull the point of the paper against the stitching, and it should pop off easily.

Removing paper

Once the paper is removed, press the stitching to set the seam, open the triangle unit, and press to the dark triangle. Starch lightly and press dry. Trim the points and measure for accuracy.

We have included a paper guide for you to try this with just in case you do not have any triangle paper available. Photocopy and enlarge it 133% onto legal-size paper. Cut 2 pieces of fabric 6″ × 14″ to get 16 units. Layer the 2 fabrics together and sew on all dotted lines, following the arrows. Rotary cut on all the solid lines and tear the paper away. Press and trim your 16 half-square triangle units.

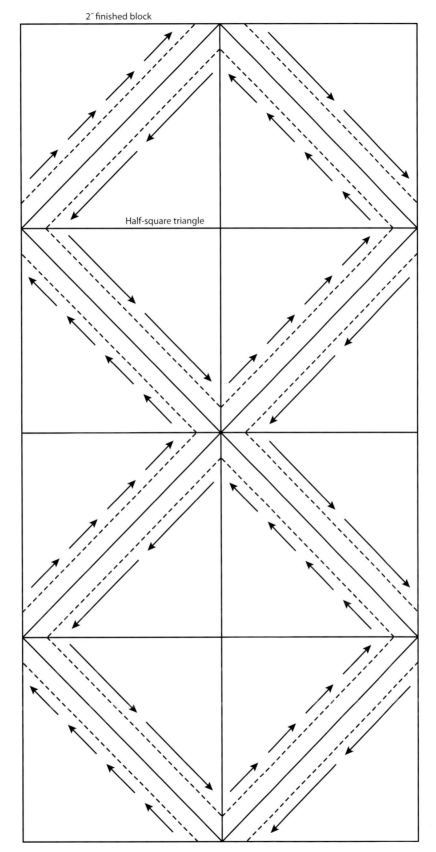

2″ finished block

Half-square triangle

Sample for paper foundation triangles

LESSON SIX:

The quilts

CARRIE'S POINSETTIA CHRISTMAS TABLE RUNNER

Carrie's Poinsettia Christmas Table Runner

Quilt top size: 93″ × 35½″

Grid size: 2″

Blocks: 8

Yardages for quilt top:

½ yard or a fat quarter each of a red and a green fabric

1 yard cream fabric

⅛ yard (or scraps) dark green for sashing

1 yard large-print fabric for setting triangles and border

Carrie designed this lovely table runner for two reasons. First, so you would have a pretty "quilt" to make after you persevered through making all those half-square triangle units from the different methods, and second, so you would have a refresher for Volume 2. The blocks are all set on point, and because of the "odd" configuration of the quilt, this will be a good challenge for you. But we know you are up to the task!

To start, you need to gather up all your envelopes or plastic bags with your various triangle units in them. Next, sort them by color for both the green blocks and the red blocks. Remember that the green block units should all have their seam allowances pressed to the green and the red blocks should have their seam allowances pressed open.

To learn the basics of constructing the 2 types of blocks that we illustrated for you in Class 310, you will be making the Pinwheel block and the Whirlwind block. Both of these blocks are good learning blocks for sewing your first half-square triangle blocks together!

To start, lay out 1 set of the green half-square triangle units as shown in the following illustration. Do you see how the quadrants of this block are identical?

Pinwheel block

Once your units are laid out, pick them back up, but in the order they are going to be sewn. Because the quadrants are all the same, you will construct all of these blocks in fourths and then sew that set of four together. Easy enough, right?

Stack the units that match the top left corner of the block illustration. In the case of this block, that will be the top left corner of each pinwheel or the third unit in the first row and the first and third units in the third row. Stack all of those matching units on top of one another. If one of them doesn't match, the block was not laid out correctly, or you turned the unit as you picked it up. Watch this, especially as you get to the other blocks that are mirror images of one another.

Next, stack all the units that match the second unit on the left in the top row. Follow that by stacking the units that match Unit 1 in Row 2. Finally, stack all 4 units that match Unit 2 in Row 2. You should now have 4 stacks of 4 units each, and these should make a pinwheel.

Stacks of units for block 1

Transport these stacks to your sewing machine, and let's start constructing. Pick up a unit from the stack for Unit 2 in Row 1, and put it right sides together with a unit from the stack on the top left. (Remember two on top of one?) This is where the extra step comes in—you need to make sure that the seams for each of these units butt up perfectly with one another. Take your time and make sure that the seams nest down the entire length of the unit. You may want to pin if you are concerned about getting the units under your machine with the seams still aligned.

Seams nested and ready to sew

Sew the seam and then pick up the next pair to sew. Depending on what makes sense to you, you can either sew all the Unit 1 and 2 pairings from

Row 1 together, or you can alternate between the Row 1 units and those in Row 2 so that you are constructing the pinwheels. Either way, there is no right or wrong; just make sure you are consistent in whichever way you decide to construct your quadrants. Chain sew these pairings together. Take your chain of units to the ironing board and cut them apart, putting them in stacks of like units, 4 in one stack and 4 in another.

Two-piece units sorted, stacked, and ready to press

Now it's time to press. Just as when you constructed the four-patch units from Volume 1 (page 56) and Volume 2 (page 49), you need to make sure your seam allowances are pressed to oppose one another so that they will nest together in the next step. Decide which direction makes sense to you and press your seam allowances, in one direction for the first stack and the opposite direction for the second stack.

Take these back to your machine to sew them together. You now have 3 seam allowances to match up, and pins will be your friend here. You need to first match and nest the vertical seams, and then you need to make sure that the diagonal seams of each of the facing units also align. By making sure all the seams butt and align, you will ensure that you do not lose or "float" a point on your triangles.

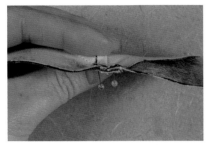

Seams nested, pinned, and ready to sew

Chain sew these pieces together and then take them to the ironing board. Fan your seams (for a reminder, see Volume 1, Class 150, page 58), press, and starch your seam allowances. You now have your 4 quadrants. Lay them out next to your sewing machine so they match your block layout. You can now assemble the block.

Four quadrants laid out

Starting with the top 2 sections, you are again going to align all the seams that come together—the horizontal seam first and then the 2 diagonal seams. Pin if necessary. Stitch these together and then pick up the second 2 sections, match all the seams, and sew.

Off to the ironing board—again you are going to have to decide which direction you want to press these seams. One needs to go one direction, and the other the opposite direction. Press and starch your block halves.

Now for the final seam—you have 7 seams to align, but if you have done this all along, they should line up perfectly without much fuss. Pin the straight seams if necessary and stitch this final seam. When you take it to the ironing board, you will want to again fan your seam allowances and starch your block. And you have 1 block done!

Back of the Pinwheel block with seam allowances fanned

This block was relatively simple in that it didn't really matter which direction you turned the finished quadrants when you were done with them; the pinwheel design in each is completely symmetrical. The rest of the blocks are not quite that easy. They are all made up of the same small blocks (the 4 units that make up the quadrant), but the quadrants are all mirror images of one another.

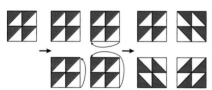

Mirror imaging a quadrant to create the block

Let's make one of the blocks with a "solid" center square. These blocks are a little different from the one you just got done with. Very few of the seams actually nest together; they generally oppose one another or make an X when they are stacked together to sew. Because of this, it can be easier to construct these blocks by using units that have their seams pressed open—which is what we are going to

do! Pick up your envelope or plastic bag that has the units you constructed from cutting around the templates (Method #3). Start as we did before and lay the block out according to the following illustration.

Whirlwind block

This is a good place to play around with your color placement—do you want the dark where it is indicated in the illustration, or would you like it to be the opposite, with the light creating the "design" in the block? Flip your units around until you like the color placement. You will quickly decide which colorway you like best. Once you have that decided and your block is laid out, you are again going to pick up the units in each quadrant to sew them together.

This is where it gets just a little tricky. Leave the first quadrant in place where it is and use that as your guide for stacking up the rest. To pick up Quadrant 2, the first unit you are going to pick up is the one that matches the top left unit in Quadrant 1. That would be the unit in the corner, but you are going to have to turn it 90° to the left to make it match. The second unit in your example quadrant is Unit 2 in Row 1. This matches the very last unit in Row 2, but that unit again needs to be turned 90° to the left. See the pattern? The third unit is Unit 1 in Row 2, which matches Unit 3 in Row 1, again turned 90°. Finally, the last unit is the third unit in Row 2. It will go on top of the second unit in the same row, but turned 90° to the left.

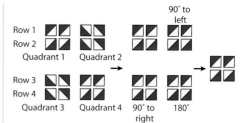

Picking up the mirror-imaged quadrants

Repeat this for each of the other 2 units. Quadrant 3 will have units that need to be turned 90° to the right to match the first quadrant. Quadrant 4 will need to have its units turned 180° to match those already in the stack.

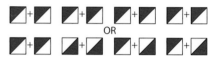

Picking up units in each quadrant to sew

Now you can sew these just as you did before—all 4 pairs from each row at a time or a pair from Row 1 and then a pair from Row 2. Once these are sewn together, take them to the ironing board and press them, again deciding the direction your seams need to go to nest together nicely.

Now you are going to sew these sets of rows together, and here is where these blocks can be a problem if you have your seams pressed to one side. You need to make sure that you either don't lose your points or that you don't float them by having an extra bit of background fabric showing.

Lost point   Floating point

When you align the rows to one another, nest the horizontal seam and then stick a pin through your pieces right where the stitching line crosses the seamline that is pressed open, or right at the color division. Check to see that the pin is bisecting both the seam you just sewed and where the two colors divide.

Using pin to check point alignment

Once you are satisfied that everything is aligned, secure with a pin carefully so that the pin does not cause any distortion. Note: This is where you will like the Clover Patchwork Pins. They are superfine, *very* sharp, and don't create distortion when you're doing precise pinning.

Make sure your horizontal seam is still butted and then align the outer edges of your units. This is where using the Marti Michell's templates or the Corner Trimmer is extremely useful. The blunted corners should line up perfectly. Once you have everything aligned, stitch this seam. When you get to where your pin is holding the point for alignment, hit that spot dead-on. This stitching line should cross right at the point where the stitching of the last seam crossed the color change of the 2 halves of the unit.

Stitching alignment with previous seam and color change of unit

Stitch all 4 of these seams, take them to your ironing board, fan your seams, and press and starch your quadrants.

Finally, you are ready to construct the block.

Lay out the quadrants. This should be considerably easier than picking them up in units. You are looking to create a solid square of color in the center.

Using the same steps as above, align the horizontal seams first, check the point alignment with a pin, adjust as needed, secure the pin, align the outer edges, and then sew the 2 sets of 2 quadrants together. At the ironing board, decide on the pressing direction of your seam allowances. Press and starch. Sew the final seam; then fan the seams, press, and starch. You are done!

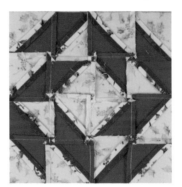
Back of Whirlwind block

Now you can continue on, using these basic instructions to construct your other chosen blocks. Look again at the illustrations on page 18 and choose 3 more of the blocks with a solid-colored center and 3 or 4 blocks with pinwheel centers—3 if you are making the table runner, 4 if you are making the square sampler quilt in the next Class (page 40).

To complete the table runner, you will start by sewing the sashing between the 4 center red blocks and then sew the center section together. This sashing finishes at 1″ wide.

Next, you will need to add the border all the way around this four-block unit. You can make your border as wide or narrow as you wish. Carrie's is 3″ after being quilted and trimmed.

Once your center section is completed, you will need to make the 2 end units. You will need 4 side-setting triangles for each unit. To determine the size of the squares you will need to cut to create the triangles, refer to Volume 2, Class 230, Lesson Three (page 38). Your blocks should finish at 8″.

Attach the setting triangles to the green squares. One triangle will go on the left side of 2 of the squares, the other 2 squares will get a square on 2 sides, and the remaining 2 triangles will be sewn to the right side of the top and bottom of the center square.

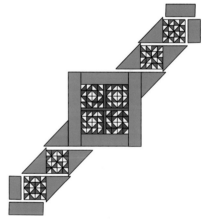
Table runner units ready to sew together

The last step to complete your table runner will be to cut the end border strips. One strip on each end needs to be cut the length of the blocks plus 2″ for trimming on the diagonal; the other strips on each end are the width of the block plus the width of the border strip already sewn on and the extra 2″ for trimming on the diagonal.

HARRIET'S VINTAGE RAINBOW BROKEN DISHES

Quilt top size: 52″ × 52″

Grid size: 2″

Blocks: 169

Layout: 13 rows of 13 blocks

Yardages for quilt top:

¼ yard or a fat quarter each of 22 different fabrics

2¼ yards background fabric

1 yard border fabric, if cut crosswise and spliced, *or* 1¾ yards lengthwise border stripe

Harriet chose to use the Eight from a Square technique taught earlier in Lesson Four for this quilt top. Please choose any one of the techniques you have learned so far if you prefer one over the Eight from a Square method. The instructions are, however, for the Eight from a Square method. We selected 22 different fabrics and cut 4 – 6″ squares from each fabric. This will give you 32 half-square units for each fabric, or 8 Broken Dishes units for each fabric.

Broken Dishes single unit

Cut:

4 – 6″ squares from each of the 22 fabrics (You will have a total of 88 squares.)

13 – 6″ strips background fabric. Subcut these strips into 7 – 6″ squares each.

Using the process for making Eight from a Square half-square triangles taught in Lesson Four, prepare and stitch the 88 pairs of squares. Once

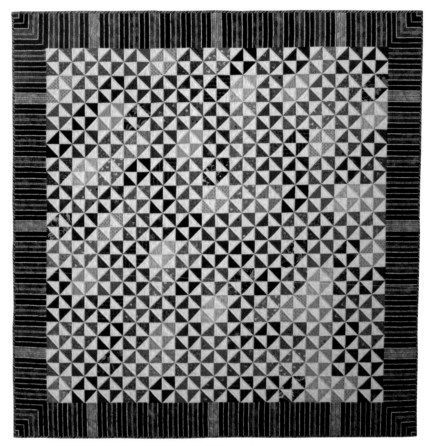

Broken Dishes quilt

they are sewn, cut the squares in half all 4 directions to get 8 half-square triangle units from each square. Press the seam allowances toward the dark triangle. Starch lightly. Trim each triangle unit to *exactly* 2½″. These units will be combined into a Broken Dishes block, using 4 units for each block.

Constructing Broken Dishes units

Each Broken Dishes unit is made up of 4 of the same half squares. Stack up the half squares needed for each unit. Refer to the illustration to the left for placement of the half-square triangles.

Start by sewing pairs of half-square triangles together. You can make 2 stacks of 16 triangle units laid out for Row 1. Row 2 is the same layout, just turned to mirror Row 1. Stitch all the pairs together, press, and then turn 8 of the pairs to form Row 2. Join the rows together.

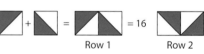

Stacks for Row 1 of Broken Dishes unit

Place 1 each of the top triangle pieces from each stack right sides together, two on top of one as you learned in Volume 1, Class 130, Lesson Six (page 29). Make sure that the entire length of the diagonal seam butts perfectly corner to corner. Double-check that the corner that will be stitched is perfectly butted. These seams need to nest together tightly so that points will be formed at these intersections. Stitch from the seam to the end of the square. Chain sew until 16 pairs are joined. Cut threads between the units and open to check that the seams come together to a point at the seamline. If there are some that don't, take the time to rip them out and try again. If this point isn't established now, there is no chance of having precise points at the next stage of joining the blocks. Press all 16 pieces toward the dark triangle.

Point formed at seamline by butting seams exactly

Next, lay out the pieces in the block formation. Refer to the Broken Dishes single unit illustration (page 32). You will have 8 joined units in each stack. Place the top Row 1 unit on top of the top Row 2 unit. This time you have 3 seams that need to butt: the center straight seam as well as the 2 diagonal seams on each side of the center seam. Again, align the diagonal seam tightly and accurately and start the seam. Butt the center seam and keep sewing, finishing the seam by aligning the final diagonal seam tightly and accurately. If you feel the need to pin, go ahead, but remember that pins can spread the seams apart if you aren't careful in their placement. (Pinning was discussed in Volume 1, Class 130, page 31.)

After you have stitched all of the units into 8 Broken Dishes units, open each unit and check that all the intersections and points are dead-on. If any are off, take the time to rip out that portion of the seam and try again.

Fan the center intersection and press this final seam. (Fanning instructions

are in Volume 1, Class 150, page 58.) Measure the block to be sure that it measures 4½″ and that the points are ¼″ from the edges.

Quilt top layout

Now the fun starts. You will be placing all of the different Broken Dishes units on the wall to create a color flow or pattern of your choice. It is always fun to see the blocks come together. The first step is to get them all up in some order and then stand back and see how you like it. You can spend quite a bit of time fussing with the placement of different colors, but it will be well worth it in the end. Below are 3 different ways to lay out the blocks. Can you come up with any others? (If you do 13 rows of 13 blocks, there will be 7 blocks leftover.)

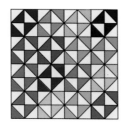

a. All blocks going same direction

b. Each block alternated, making an X pattern

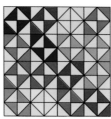

c. Each row changes directions, making a zigzag pattern.

Once you get all the blocks placed where they are the most appealing to you, it is time to join them together. Using the stacking method taught in Volume 1, Class 130 (page 29), work with 12 units to create 6 pairs, leaving 1 unit leftover at the end of each row.

   ...
Row 1   6   1

Join 12 units into 6 pairs with 1 leftover at end of row

Once 2 rows are sewn into pairs, join the 2 rows by joining 1 pair from each row into blocks of 4 Broken Dishes units.

Row 1   6 units of 4 + 1
Row 2 ...

Join pairs from 2 rows into 6 blocks of 4 units each.

When joining the first pair of Row 1 to the first pair of Row 2, we suggest that you do not pin. Align the 2 pairs, Row 1 on top. Align and butt the seams to the left of the raw edge and start stitching the right edge. Stitch about 1″ and stop with the needle in the fabric. Separate the 2 layers and visually align the upcoming seam intersection. You have 8 points coming together at one place, so try to interlock and align the points as closely as you can. If you have been very precise up to now, the raw edges should be even and the points should come together right on the spot.

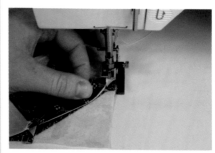

Visually aligning seam allowance to match points

Stitch through the intersection and align the next upcoming seams. This seam is a standard butted seam. After you have sewn through it, stop with the needle in the fabric and align the next intersection, again aligning all 4 points. When you arrive at the last unit, align the upcoming intersection as well as the seam to the left and at the bottom edge of the block. This ensures that the corner is square and the seam allowance is accurate. Once the seam is finished, open the block and closely check the intersections. Make any corrections necessary to make the points align into precise pinwheels with 8 sharp points.

Broken Dishes units combined into fours

Continue joining the rows into pairs and making 2 rows of pairs into blocks of 4 units, or 2 pairs each.

You now have 6 rows, each having 6 of the 4-piece units, with 1 unit left-over on the right side and individual units in the thirteenth row. You can sew the 13 separate units together into 1 row at this time.

Join pairs together.

Once all the blocks are sewn into combined units of 4, press the seams, fanning the seam allowances again. Next, combine the 4-unit pieces into 16-unit blocks. You should now have 3 rows of 3 large blocks each.

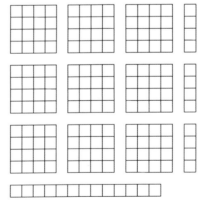

Three rows of 3 large blocks

Join the single pairs that are at the end of the rows into units that are 2 long and add them to the side of the third large block. You can now sew the 3 rows together, pressing after each long seam is sewn. Add the thirteenth row last. As you combine all the units, you will suddenly have a complete quilt top. It seems that you sew forever on the smaller units, and then all of a sudden, they all come together as large units quickly.

Once the top is completed, measure both sides to be sure they are exactly the same length and measure the top and bottom to check they are the same width. The quilt top should be 52″ square at this point. If any of the sides are not the correct width or length, find the seams that are causing the problem and correct them as we discussed in Volume 1, Class 180, Lesson One (page 93). Once the quilt top is perfectly square, add any type of border you desire. Harriet added a single border using the fabric that inspired the color palette for this quilt. The border was cut 8″ and will be cut down to finish at 6″ after the quilting is completed.

Class 330

Designing with linking blocks

There are many linking blocks, also known as connector blocks, that can be pieced and connected to other pieced blocks for an unexpected effect. In Volume 1, we used a simple linking block in the Double Irish Chain, and in Volume 2, they showed up in the Five-Patch Chain and the Four-Patch Chain patterns. These were basic blocks using squares. With the addition of triangles, these blocks can create a lot of excitement when used in the design phase. Typical blocks that can be used to link or connect may include those in the following illustrations. Depending on the design block used, these blocks may or may not create a secondary design. Note that these blocks can be redrafted to different grids to fit your design block. These illustrations are to generate ideas only. They are neither the only blocks that can be used nor the only grid that can be used.

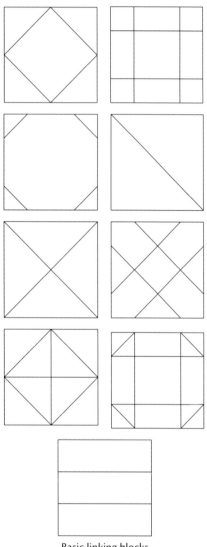

Basic linking blocks

One of the most basic and common linking blocks is the Snowball block. It is probably the most-used linking block of them all. This block can transform a quilt in many ways, as the following illustrations show.

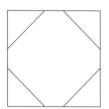

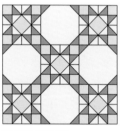

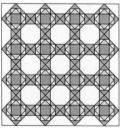

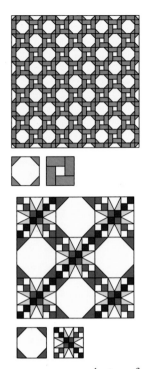

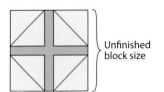

Unfinished block size

Corner square placement

Sew on the fold or the line of each square. You can do this efficiently by turning the block for each corner without cutting the threads.

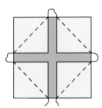

Sew on line.

Trim away the outside corners of each square ¼" beyond the stitching. Do not cut away the background corner. When the triangle is turned back and pressed, make sure that the corners are the same and the block is square. Once this is done, the background corner can be cut away if you choose.

More complicated linking blocks

Here are more blocks that are a bit more complicated that you can use in the same way. They are fun to play with.

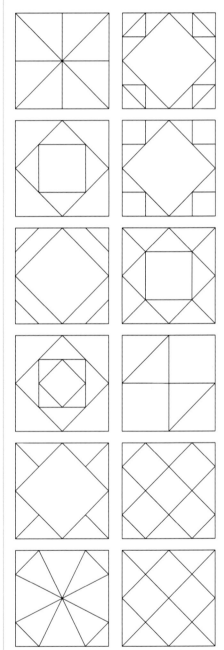

More complicated linking blocks

The most common technique for making this block is known as "cheater corners" or "folded square corners." Start by completing your design blocks. Turn a block over to the wrong side and measure raw edge to raw edge of the unit you want your triangle corner to line up to. Cut a strip of fabric that will be used for the corner the same width as this measurement. Cut the strip into squares. These will become your triangle corners. Either fold in half diagonally and press in a crease line or lightly draw a diagonal line corner to opposite corner on the wrong side of the square.

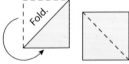

Fold in half. Draw line.

From the background fabric, cut squares for the connector block the same size as the design block. Place the smaller squares on each corner, making sure that the diagonal lines form a circle.

tip If you have collected any of the Perfect Patchwork Templates, you can easily use them for this block. Instead of cutting squares, find the template that is the correct size for the corner of the block you are making. When you lay the template on the large snowball square, you will see that the cut corners align with the edge of the block. Cut the triangles using the template, align with the square corner for placement, and sew your seam allowance. Press and trim away the corner of the square.

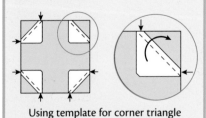

Using template for corner triangle

An excellent exercise is to take different design blocks and draw them on graph paper, using any of the illustrated linking blocks as alternate blocks. Use the worksheets in Volume 2, Class 250, as well as the graph paper designed to go along with the worksheets (see Resources, page 128) to also incorporate setting options in your designing. The possibilities will seem endless. You will start to see how much interaction happens between the two and see if a secondary design emerges. Work with an arrangement of at least three blocks by three blocks. Don't forget that color placement can really play a role when working with these blocks, as you will see in Lesson Five.

We hope you enjoy playing with the concept of linking blocks. The possibilities are endless, and the more you play, the more you'll see that wonderfully intricate quilts can often be achieved by simple pieced blocks and strategic color placement. Taking the time to experiment and play will lead you to designing original patterns and will make your quilt tops uniquely yours. One of our biggest goals with this series of books is that you learn to design original quilts and start to get away from relying on kits and patterns for everything you make.

LESSON TWO:

Using triangles in block framing

We discussed framing with coping strips in Volume 2, Class 240. We used the coping strips to make blocks of different sizes able to be squared to one size. Now think of this in a different application. Instead of simple strips surrounding the block, what if we used pieced units that would create another element of design to the overall effect of the blocks. Attic Window, Square in a Square, and the use of setting squares are a few examples.

 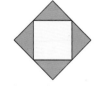

Attic Window   Square in a Square   Setting Squares

Another simple way to create a pieced frame for your block is to imagine what an Ohio Star (or any other block) set inside a Sawtooth Star might look like, or how about inside a Lady of the Lake block?

 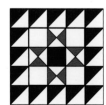

Ohio Star in a   Ohio Star in a
Sawtooth Star frame   Lady of the Lake frame

Any block that has a blank area in the center can serve as a great frame for other blocks. For that matter, you can simply remove piecing structure from a block and substitute something else for what was there originally.

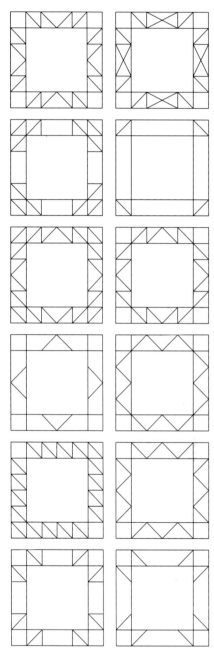

Options for pieced frames

In order to create these more involved elements, you need to understand the basic components. They aren't hard, but if you don't know how to break down the block, you're going to find it difficult to create intricate sets. If you skipped the basic drafting information in Volume 1, Class 150, we suggest that you go back and review it so that you have a firm understanding of grids and changing sizes of them to accommodate your needs.

Let's work through a simple example. If you want to put a 6″ Ohio Star block inside a 10″ Sawtooth Star block, how can you make that happen? Framing strips! A 10″ Sawtooth Star has an 8″ square in the center. If you sew strips to the 6″ Ohio Star block and square it to 8½″ (remember, that includes the seam allowance), then you can do it. If you don't want framing strips, then you would have a finished 9″ Sawtooth Star for the frame of our 6″ block. You would be changing grid size for the Sawtooth Star from a 2½″ grid for the 10″ block to a 2¼″ grid for the 9″ block. Both are quilter friendly numbers, so the decision is based on your personal taste and needs.

Ohio Star with framing strips in a Sawtooth Star block

LESSON THREE:

Square in a Square block

The Square in a Square block is a wonderful linking block as well as design block. It is a versatile block to use with small panel prints, embroidered squares, or anything else you want to frame on point.

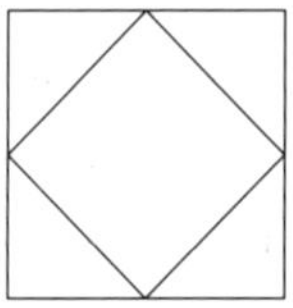

Square in a Square block

You are likely to encounter problems making this block with units cut to size. The triangles on the outside have a tendency to get a bow along the outside edge, making them too small and the sides not square and straight. Therefore, we are going to walk you through a method of using triangles that are larger than they should be, and then trim them down to the exact size needed.

Start by cutting the triangles that will go around the center square. You want to cut them larger than the pattern you are working with or your drafted design calls for. If the pattern asks you to cut the triangles from a square, add ½″ to the measurement given. That gives each triangle an extra ¼″ as a margin for error.

You can either rotary cut the triangles or use the Easy Angle ruler to do this. We prefer to simply cut squares and cut them in half to get triangles. Use the following chart if you want an easy reference for cut sizes.

Square in a Square cutting sizes

Finished size	Center square	Rotary cut square (cut in half)
2″	1⅞″	2⅜″
2½″	2⅛″	2½″
3″	2⅝″	2⅞″
3½″	3″	3¼″
4″	3⅜″	3⅜″
4½″	3⅝″	3½″
5″	4″	3⅝″
5½″	4⅜″	4″
6″	4¾″	4⅜″

Now for the steps to creating an accurate 3″ Square in a Square block:

Cut the center square 2⅝″.

1. Cut 4 triangles from a 2½″ strip of fabric and use the Easy Angle 2½″ measure to cut with. If you don't have an Easy Angle ruler, you can do this the traditional way. Cut 2 – 2⅞″ squares and carefully cut them corner to corner diagonally.

2. Fold the center square in half and lightly crease. This line will be used to position the first 2 triangles.

3. Position the first triangle along the cut edge of the square, making sure that the point of the triangle is exactly on the crease line of the square. Stitch. Do not press yet.

4. Position the second triangle opposite the first, repeating the process above.

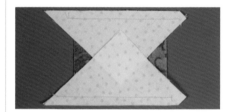

Placement of first 2 triangles

5. Press both triangle points and starch lightly.

6. Using a ruler, trim off the points so they are straight with the remaining edges of the square. This will help keep the next triangles aligned with the square when sewing.

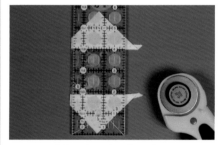

Trimming triangle points

7. Crease the centerline into the square again, this time in the opposite direction.

8. Repeat the process above for adding the remaining 2 triangles.

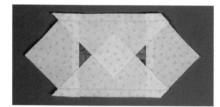
Adding remaining triangles

9. We use the Precision Trimmer to trim away the extra and to get a ¼″ seam allowance beyond the points. Use the ¼″ lines around the perimeter of the ruler. Place the ¼″ line on 2 sides, as shown in the photo below. Align the inner lines of the ruler with the points of the inside square and any other lines that help you keep the square exact. Trim. Repeat for the opposite corner. Your block should be exactly 3½″ square after trimming. If it is not, check your seam allowances.

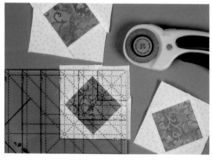
Trimming to size

note We suggest that you make a sample of the block you need to ensure that your seam allowance is correct for the technique. If your seam allowance is too wide, the square will be too small. If your seam allowance is too small, the square will be too large, and you will lose the points of the square when the triangles are trimmed.

LESSON FOUR:
Using triangles to design sashing

SASHING USING FOLDED CORNERS (SAWTOOTH STAR SASHING)

A very easy and effective design is the Sawtooth Star sashing. This incorporates sashing and cornerstones into a Sawtooth Star pattern that appears each time four quilt blocks intersect. The following illustration shows an example of this sashing.

Sawtooth Star sashing

You'll need 2 fabrics for the sashing and only 2 measurements—the length of one side of a quilt block and the width of the sashing that you choose to use.

We are using the same corner triangle method we did with the Snowball block. You need to cut squares equal to half the width of the finished size of the sashing plus ½″.

Measuring for corner squares

Once the squares are cut, fold them in half diagonally and press. Position the new triangle in the corner of the rectangular sashing strip and

open; then sew on the fold line. Press toward the corner and trim out the back of the square. Repeat with the opposite corner, and then the other end. The back part of the square can be cut away, but you can leave the sashing intact for stability.

Position of corner squares   Trimming and folding corners

tip Don't forget that you can also use templates to cut a triangle that fits this corner exactly if you don't care for the folded square or are having problems with accuracy with this technique.

The cornerstone will be cut from the same fabric as the star points. Cut them to the cut width of the sashing. Once the strips have the points attached, connect them in the same manner as sashing with cornerstones. Once all the sashing is joined to the blocks, Sawtooth Stars will appear at every intersection.

Connect sashing to blocks

You can adapt this method to resemble latticework sashing without piecing the cornerstone. Start by adding a framing strip around all 4 sides of all blocks. Keep the size of these strips proportional to the block. Continue with the Sawtooth Star sashing technique. Because the corners connect with the framing strips, you get latticework instead of stars.

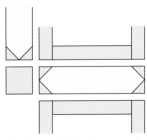

Breakout piecing of Sawtooth
Star/latticework variation

Sawtooth Star/latticework variation
is a common setting treatment
for appliqué blocks.

Sampler quilt with Sawtooth sashing

LATTICEWORK SASHING

This sashing is the same as strip sashing with cornerstones, but instead of a plain or pieced block for the cornerstone, the square changes to an X. You'll see this sashing used very effectively with many appliquéd or embroidered blocks. Proportion is very important for this sashing. If the latticework is heavy (wide), it may overwhelm a simple pattern, but if it's too dainty (narrow), it can be overwhelmed by a bold design. You will need to play with widths for your specific design. This is a good exercise for you to become comfortable with your visual preferences regarding width (weight) of sashing and borders. There really is no right or wrong—only what looks good to you!

For this exercise, the lattice will be made from two outer 1″ strips and

one inner 2″ strip, giving a 4″ finished sashing strip.

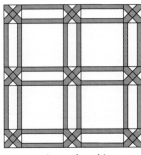

Latticework sashing

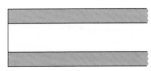

Strips for sashing

To create templates for a cornerstone, draw a 4″ square on a piece of graph paper. From each corner, mark the width of the outside sashing strip in both directions. Our measurement is 1″. Next, connect these marks diagonally in both directions.

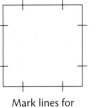

Mark lines for latticework.   Connect lines.

This will give you the template pieces needed to construct the square. Remember that C is the inner strip fabric of the sashing and A and B match the outside strips. Seam allowances need to be added to each shape.

This can also be achieved by piecing three pieces together and then appliquéing a strip finished to the size of the diagonal unit on top of the square. Trim the corners.

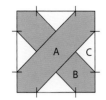

Identify template shapes

Sew three pieces together.

Appliqué strip

If this seems like a lot of work, refer to Sawtooth Star sashing above to find another way of achieving a similar latticework look.

PIECED SASHING

One very simple pieced sashing has already been addressed when we talked about the Sawtooth Star set at the beginning of this lesson. Another very simple pieced sash creates a Friendship Star block at all the sashed intersections.

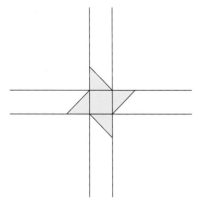

Friendship Star sashing

Your sashing can be divided into much more complicated structures and then colored to create even more variations. How do you begin this process? The answer again is graph paper. Start with a piece of graph paper and draw a rectangle equal to the width and length of the finished sash. If you have 9″ blocks and you're planning a 3″ sash (which is actually a very pleasing scale when pieced), then start with a 3″ × 9″ rectangle. Nine inches divides equally by 1″, 1½″, 3″, and 4½″. Using these numbers, see what designs you can come up with.

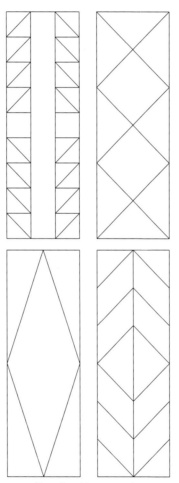

Pieced sashing examples

Once you've determined the design, play with coloration. If you photocopy your design and work strictly in value (light, medium, and dark), you can get a feel for what might happen to the design simply by reversing the position of light and dark.

Designing with triangles

Creativity—a state when you forget about yourself—you are having so much fun you want to elongate the moment—you're more present—not rushing.—Dr. Joe Dispenza

If you really want to have fun learning to design your own original quilts, there are systems that use the simple half-square unit in groups that can create a multitude of different designs. There are also basic design principles that make original design much easier than you might think. The first four lessons of this class asked you to start playing with simple elements like linking blocks and sashing. This is just the beginning. If you had a formula that walked you through a number of exercises, do you think you could come up with something unique and original? We think so!

The 1980s were an amazing time period for quilting. After 60 years of dormancy everything seemed new and exciting; people's imaginations were in high gear; and the result was fast sewing techniques, design ideas, new ways of thinking about quilts, and the freedom to express ourselves in fabrics we had never had available before. By the 1990s, the industry had grown beyond what anyone expected, and we are still experiencing a strong growth. We believe the reason quilting never seems to slow down is technology. We are not giving it credit for the progress, but instead giving it credit for driving people, mainly women, back to using their hands and minds to create something of use and beauty. After a day in front of a cold, impersonal computer at the office, we yearn to do something creative with our minds. Even though the computer has crept into quilting through Electric Quilt and other design programs, how many of us really want to sit behind a computer in our free time and not really produce anything of our own doing at the end of the session? Not us—we need a new quilt or new placemats or something fabric to satisfy that need to create. We want to engage our minds and our hands simultaneously.

Creativity is becoming a lost art. It seems that the majority of quilters now feel that a few have the ability to create, and the rest of us will buy their patterns, kits, and books and rely on them to do the work, so we can just do the sewing. The trend is to not choose our own fabric, but buy a kit, and to not even do our own quilting anymore! Can you imagine the sense of satisfaction and passion you would have for a quilt that you designed, pieced, and quilted yourself! Do you think this is beyond you? Think again—it is as simple as a pad of graph paper and a box of colored pencils.

Books that started an industry

In 1982 one of the most innovative and inspiring people to enter the quilting scene was Mary Ellen

Hopkins. She burst onto the scene with ideas that had you losing sleep. When *The It's Okay If You Sit On My Quilt Book* was released in 1982, Mary Ellen was teaching weeklong seminars for shop owners that created an industry. Most of today's newer quilters don't know about Mary Ellen, but if anyone kept this industry excited in the early revival years, it was Mary Ellen. You can trace the history of many of today's designers and innovators back to Mary Ellen's seminars—including Harriet. (Equal credit must be given here to Marti Michell, who developed the seminars. She is truly one of the very first innovators of the quilt revival and is still going strong!) Shop owners and teachers showed up with a sewing machine, 50 yards of fabric, and the willingness to share and develop as much as possible in 5 days and nights of endless sewing and sharing. *The It's Okay If You Sit On My Quilt Book* is a book where the blocks are printed on graph paper so you can automatically see the grid and shapes within each square. If you don't have a copy of this book, you might find it helpful with your designing adventure. It is the first book off the shelf when Harriet and Carrie need to find a block or an idea.

In 1987, Barbara Johannah, the pioneer of quick quiltmaking, wrote a book titled *Half Square Triangles: Exploring Design* (ISBN 0-934342-04-0). This book is a wonderful resource for working with the thousands of possible combinations of half-square triangles. It is where the idea of working with mirrors to see the design repeat got off the ground. In the book is Jane Warnick's Element Key with 256 different ways

to manipulate groups of 4 half-square triangle units into an unlimited number of half-square triangle patterns. This concept was repeated again in Barbara's book *Barbara Johannah's Crystal Piecing* (ISBN 0-8019-8400-9), which was released in 1993.

Harriet's book *Heirloom Machine Quilting* was also printed in 1987. This book has been in continual print since then and is the book that changed the course of the actual quilting aspect of quiltmaking forever. Once we began to make quilt tops at the speed of light, the next problem was to keep up with the quilting. The sewing machine was the answer, and Harriet was the teacher. She worked with Mary Ellen for a couple of years to teach shop owners how to pass on the skill and keep people excited about making more and more quilts. Harriet finds it extremely disappointing that now we have taken the easy way out and don't design our own quilts. We instead buy kits and jelly rolls, charm packs and patterns by the dozens, and we don't even consider learning the skill of quilting, because we can so simply send it out to the longarm quilter. Where is the imagination in all this? Where is the sense of accomplishment and pride in the creation of an item? Has quiltmaking just become an activity that simply creates a reason to shop and spend money? What kind of legacy are we leaving to our families—Mom sewed the fabric together, but someone else did everything else? We are hoping that you get excited enough to take a breath; slow down; get a cup of tea, your graph paper, and pencils; and start to take the journey into creativity. You are beginning an adventure that will have you in that wonderful part of the brain that puts all the stresses of life to the side and allows you to get lost in time. Have fun with this.

HALF-SQUARE TRIANGLES

The earliest record, and perhaps the rarest book, on the theory of design shows us a method of arranging half-square triangles into endless combinations or permutations. This concept has its origin in the early eighteenth century with a French monk named Pere Dominique Douat. He was fascinated with designs that could be made with light and dark half-square triangles. He worked with tiles to find all the possible design variations within a given framework. In 1704 the Royal Academy of Sciences in Paris published a paper on Douat's infinite system of design. In 1979, a book named *The Sense of Order* by E. H. Gombrich was published, presenting several illustrations and a mention of Douat's system.

The first table on the page shown below explains the method and the symbolism. By rotating the half-square triangles, four variants are produced. These are marked with the first four letters of the alphabet. The second table shows sets of two such variants resulting in sixteen possibilities.

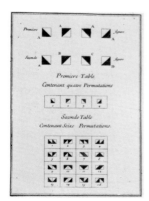

Photos of first page from Pere Douat's book

Douat made up tables of symbols of all the combinations he discovered that could be made by this simple shape.

Tables that show Douat's method of permutation

His findings resulted in sets of 3 that give 64 permutations; sets of 4 give 256 permutations. This kept multiplying until you discover that it goes into infinity.

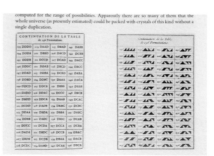

Example of a page from Douat's book showing combinations

Another page showing variations of the combinations

A quilter named Jane Warnick came across these pages and was inspired to apply the system to quilting. She thought the illustrations in the previous papers looked like quilts just waiting to be made. With the quick triangle piecing method developed by both Ernest Haight and Barbara Johannah (independently of each other), she began her exploration of the system. She developed The Half-Square Triangle Element Key, which was published in Barbara Johannah's book *Half Square Triangles: Exploring Design* as well as in *Barbara Johannah's Crystal Piecing*. Instead of placing the units in a straight row of four, she organized them into units of two rows of two elements each.

Jane Warnick's Half Square Triangle Element Key

Working with the elements can create thousands of patterns. The easiest way to get started in this adventure is to make up paper half-square triangle units. Draw 2″ squares on graph paper and color in one half to make half-square triangle units. Make at least 36. Start laying out 1 triangle element from Jane Warnick's Element Key. Element 185 is what we chose to illustrate. The secret to using these elements is to rotate them within a square. It will take 16 half-square triangle pieces to complete this exercise.

Element 185

Draw an 8″ square on graph paper. Begin placing the element in one corner and rotate the element one-quarter at a time to fill all four corners.

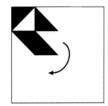 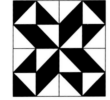

Original element, rotating within square, final block

Does this block look familiar? It is the Barbara Frietchie star that is a part of the sampler quilt table runner you made in Class 320. If you study all the blocks in the sampler, you will be able to find the original element that was rotated to create the block. Can you find the elements that make up the other blocks in the sampler?

Using mirrors is another one of Barbara Johannah's great ideas. You can see an element repeated by using mirrors—mirror imaging. Make up one element using your paper triangles, marking each of the four corners with A, B, C, and D. Place the mirrors in one corner of your design element, and you will see in the reflection the element repeated three more times. Now move the mirror to each of the other three corners, and you will find three more totally different designs emerge. Next, try placing the mirrors through the middle at a 45° angle. Keep moving the mirrors around on the element, and you will see many different patterns emerge.

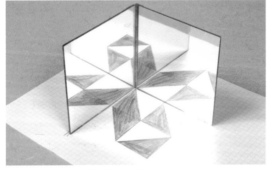

Working with mirrors

Women in the past have already discovered hundreds of these patterns, such as Yankee Puzzle, Hopscotch, Anna's Choice, Clay's Star, Whirligig, and most of the star patterns using triangles, just to name a few. Fourteen of such blocks are illustrated on page 18. Can you locate the original element and how it is turned or repeated to develop each block? Take some time to play with these ideas. You

might come up with something so exciting that you want to build on it and start to design your first original quilt top!

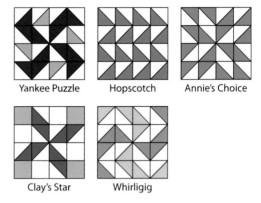

Yankee Puzzle   Hopscotch   Annie's Choice

Clay's Star   Whirligig

MARY ELLEN'S TWO-BELL BLOCKS

Building on this idea, Mary Ellen Hopkins came up with her idea of two-bell blocks. In her book *The It's Okay If You Sit On My Quilt Book,* which came out in 1982, in a chapter titled "Secrets No One Ever Told You," she introduced the idea of designing new or different patterns using two elements found in blocks that already exist. What are the bells? What goes off in your head when you see one of these designs? Read on.

The first element (the first bell) is a block that has a diagonal line through it that is easy for the eye to identify. This creates the half-square triangle idea. The diagonal line creates two sides, like a Log Cabin block. There is a light and a dark side. Or a heavier and lighter side. Any block with the word *Road* in it has the diagonal line in it. All of these blocks can be pivoted around to create secondary designs.

The second element (the second bell) to look for is that the block has at least two different corners. These two bells are what create the secondary designs we are looking for.

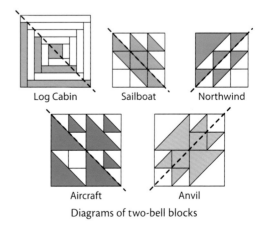

Log Cabin   Sailboat   Northwind

Aircraft   Anvil

Diagrams of two-bell blocks

CREATING DESIGNS WITH THE TWO ELEMENTS

You will need graph paper, colored pencils, and a set of design mirrors. Be prepared to get lost in this process. You can become so entranced with the possibilities that you lose all track of time! What fun!!

Using a two-bell block, start by drawing 4 blocks that are the same on graph paper. Draw these blocks to be about 4″ square. Color them in black and white to see the design emerge. You can use color later when you have a design you really like. Photocopy them several times so that you have several of each little block. Start to play with them by twisting and turning the blocks together. You might want to use your digital camera to keep a record of each different design for future reference.

Photo of paper blocks on cutting table

Once you get the idea of how these blocks work, challenge yourself by drawing more blocks but not filling in any of the triangles. You will just have the blocks with the diagonal lines drawn in. Make up a design that uses 4 (2 × 2), 9 (3 × 3), or 16 (4 × 4) settings. Once you have a great pattern developed, glue down the blocks and start to color.

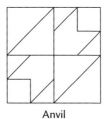

Anvil

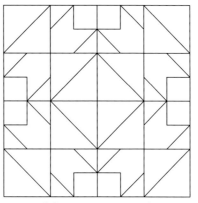

Anvil drawn into 4 × 4 patch set

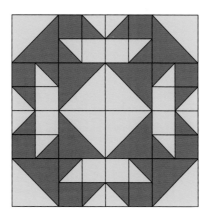

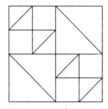

Crosses and Losses

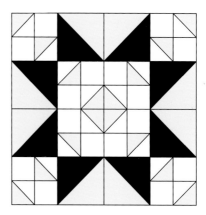

Crosses and Losses in four-patch sets

Let's get a bit more complicated. Follow along with the progression of the Hovering Hawks and the Aircraft blocks. You can photocopy the empty line drawings and do your own color versions. See how many ideas you can come up with.

Start with the basic block:

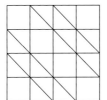

Hovering Hawks

Draw 16 blocks together.

Sixteen blocks together

Leaving the block in its original design

Taking out lines and making larger areas of color

Cleaning up even more lines for a tile effect

Less emphasis on the stars

Let's try another one, but this time we are going to eliminate even more lines in the original block and make it larger.

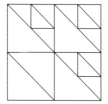

Aircraft

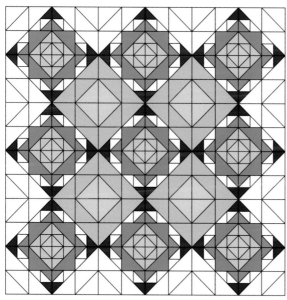

Thirty-six blocks together
Version 1

Version 2

If these ideas don't excite you about creating some original designs, we don't know what will. We hope you are starting to see that the creative process can start with a formula. Once you draw the blocks on paper, you will start to see different shapes and areas emerge. All you have to do is start to color. As you get more comfortable with drafting, you will be able to figure out the shapes and units that will be sewn together, assign a size to the grid and the finished quilt, and you are on your way!

Here are a few more blocks that work with this design principle. We hope they inspire you to play with your graph paper and colored pencils. Draw out any of these ideas onto graph paper and start to color them in, letting your imagination go. You will start to see secondary patterns emerge, and the original design lines will start to recede, giving you a whole new outlook on the design lines. Below are some other blocks to play with on your own.

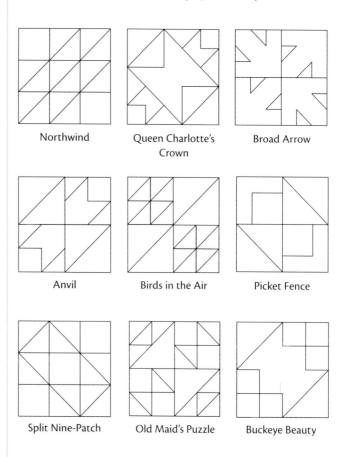

Northwind

Queen Charlotte's Crown

Broad Arrow

Anvil

Birds in the Air

Picket Fence

Split Nine-Patch

Old Maid's Puzzle

Buckeye Beauty

Can you find more blocks with the requirements of two-bell blocks?

Spring Has Sprung

LESSON SIX:
The quilts

CARRIE'S SPRING HAS SPRUNG

Quilt top size: 45″ × 45″ (without borders)

Grid size: 1½″

Blocks:

13 design blocks

12 alternate blocks

Layout: 5 rows of 5 blocks

Yardages for quilt top:

⅔ yard pink print
(if doing the sheeting method for triangles)

⅔ yard light pink solid
(if doing the sheeting method for triangles)

¾ yard green print

1⅙ yards large pink print

Are you ready for your first challenge? This quilt is it! This pretty little quilt is not for the faint of heart! It has lots of great things to learn as you make it, but we must remind you to first slow down and take your time with this one, as there are lots of points and lines to match. Second, if the small grid presents an issue, use the drafting skills you are learning and scale the whole grid up to a 2″. The skills you

learn while making this quilt will prepare you to make any Northwinds or Lady of the Lake design you may encounter in the future. They use the same techniques. So with that, let's get started!

We are going to start by constructing the design blocks. We are doing this first because much like what you learned when working with combined grids, you will want to be able to tweak your alternate blocks' size if necessary if the design blocks end up being smaller or larger than what is mathematically correct.

There are three steps to making this block. First, you are going to construct the half-square triangle units (A and B). Then, you will add the green triangles (C) and then the large pink print triangles (D), and finally, you will sew the quadrants together.

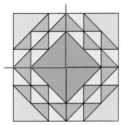

Design block with units broken out

To make the half-square triangle units, Carrie chose to use the sheeting method. If, however, this was not your favorite method for making half-square triangles, by all means, pick your favorite method from Class 310 or 320. You will need a total of 156 light pink solid and pink print units when you are finished.

To use the sheeting method, pair up 4 sets of pink print and pink solid fabric cut 11″ × 14″. Follow the instructions on pages 20 and 21 for marking your grid and sewing lines. Remember, these units will finish at 1½″, or are 2″ cut. If you are very accurate with your sewing, you only need to add ⅞″ for your seam allowances. If you would rather trim, add 1″.

Now you need to make the single triangles. You need 8 of each color (pink print and pink solid) for each design block. Carrie chose to cut hers a little large and trim them down to size once sewn to the half-square triangle units, so they ended up being completely accurate. This would be similar to the way we do the setting triangles on a diagonal set quilt. You want the straight of grain to be on the outside of your finished unit, so you will be cutting a square in half diagonally twice. To get the 8 triangles you need per block, you need to cut 2 squares. We have 13 blocks × 2 squares = 26 squares needed.

To figure out what size your squares need to be, here is the math:

You have a 1½″ grid (the finished size of the half-square triangle units). Take this times 1.414 to get the diagonal measurement: 1.5″ × 1.414 = 2.121″. Add your seam allowance of ⅞″. Here is the equation: 2.121″ + .875″ = 2.996″ or 3″. If you want to trim your pieces down as Carrie did, you will need to add ⅛″ to ¼″, depending on your level of comfort. Cut your 26 squares of each fabric and then cut them in half diagonally twice.

Now you are ready to construct the first part of the design block. Lay out your units like the following illustration and make stacks 13 deep.

Design block part 1—units laid out ready to sew

Chain sew all the pink solid triangles to the half-square triangle units. Press the seam allowance toward the single triangle. Starch and trim the triangle point off flush with the half-square triangle unit. Lay your pieces out like the previous diagram and chain sew the pink print triangles to the half-square triangles units. Press the seam again toward the triangle, starch, and trim flush.

Now you can assemble the pieces together. Start by sewing the half-square triangle / pink solid triangle

unit to the 3-piece unit. Make sure that you butt your seams well. Pin if necessary. (See Volume 1, Class 130, page 31, for pinning tips.)

This is a good place to practice fanning your seams to reduce the bulk. (See Volume 1, Class 150, page 58, for a refresher.)

Next, add the half-square triangle / pink print triangle unit to the opposite side of the 3-piece unit. Butt the seams, pin, and chain sew. Fan your seam allowances, press, and starch. Now it is time to trim.

Your units need to be 2¾″ wide—that is ¼″ from the tips of your half-square triangle points. It is easiest to trim these by aligning the ¼″ line with the very ends of those points and trimming off any extra fabric.

Trimming triangle units to size

Now you need to cut the green triangles for the design block. To determine the size you need, turn over one of the triangle units you just made. Measure from stitching line to stitching line ¼″ from the edge.

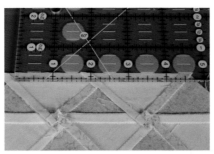

Measuring to determine size of green triangles

Did you come up with about 4½″? This is the diagonal measurement of the square you need to cut. Take 4.5 ÷ 1.414 = 3.18 or a 3⅛″ triangle, in ruler friendly language. Remember, this is your finished size, so add ⅞″ for seam allowance, which equals 4″, or for a little fudge factor, 4¼″.

If you don't understand how we got this measurement, here is another way to do it. Lay one of the triangle units out on a piece of 4-to-the-inch graph paper, aligned with the graph paper lines. Then draw a line from one straight edge of the triangle unit up a few inches and then draw a second straight line from the other straight edge until it intersects your first straight line. Make a mark where you started drawing (right next to the triangle unit), or you can draw a line exactly parallel to the raw edge of the triangle unit. Once you have all of your lines drawn, count up the number of squares from your beginning mark to where your lines meet, creating your block corner. This number will tell you the exact finished size of the square you need to cut. Once you know that size, add your seam allowance allotment and any extra for fudge room to trim your blocks to exact size.

Using graph paper to determine triangle size

With the graph paper method, you will actually come up with the finished size square—3⅛″ again. Add your seam allowance and fudge factor (if desired). You need 4 triangles per unit, and each square gives you 2 triangles when cut in half once. You have 13 design blocks—2 squares per block, or 26 squares.

To figure how many strips you need, divide your width of fabric (42″) by the size of your squares; round if necessary. Take the number of squares you need, divide by the number you just got, and that gives you the number of strips; round up.

For example, 42″ ÷ 4.25″ = 9.88 squares per strip. You can actually round this up to 10 squares because this equals 42.5″, and we are working with 44″ or 45″ fabric; you will have enough. In equation form: 26 squares total ÷ 10 = 2.6 or 3 strips, cut 4¼″ wide.

The large pink print triangles on the design blocks will be cut the same size, so cut 26 of those too.

To sew the green triangles onto the units you have already constructed, fold them in half along the long edge of the triangle and make a light crease in the middle. Line the crease up with the point of the pink print triangle; align your pin with the point of the triangle and then through the green triangle. With the green triangle toward your feed dogs, sew your seam, aiming your needle for a thread or two to the right of the spot where your pin marks the point of the triangle. This will ensure that you don't lose your points. Press toward the green triangle and starch.

Pin alignment for sewing triangles

Now mark your large pink print triangles with a crease and align that crease with the pink solid triangle point of the half-square triangle unit. Align, pin, and sew, again pressing the seam allowance toward the large pink print triangle.

Now you need to trim your quarter blocks down to size. They should measure 5″. This is a great place to use Marsha McCloskey's Precision Trimmer 6 to square up the blocks. Align the diagonal line at the 3½″ measure with the seamline of the green triangle and trim off any excess fabric. Turn your block around and do the same to the large pink print triangle.

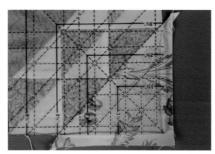
Ruler alignment for trimming quarter blocks to size

Now you are ready to assemble the block. Lay out the quarter blocks you have constructed in a stack to look like the finished block. You will have 4 stacks with 13 blocks in them. Start sewing the top 2 and bottom 2 quarter blocks together. You have 3 places where you really need to watch the alignment of your pieces. The first is where the 2 green triangles meet, the second is where the straight line is formed by the pink print triangles, and the third is where the points of the pink print triangles meet.

To get the first two lined up properly, place a pin through one of the blocks, right where the stitching of the green triangle to the half-square units intersects the horizontal stitching of the half-square triangle unit. Pin through the other unit at the exact same location and take a stitch with the pin. If you have done much garment making, this is the same thing you do when matching alignment marking on the interior of a garment. This will help to ensure that those points are as aligned with one another as possible. For the points of the pink print triangle, make sure that the seamlines are running completely parallel to one another; pin here as well.

When stitching the blocks together, stitch from the pink print triangle end toward the green. As you approach the stitching intersection you pinned, aim your needle just to the right of that intersection, even if your seam allowance ends up being a little narrower than normal. By doing this, you will ensure that you don't lose any points.

Aiming for stitching intersection

Press your seam allowance open.

Once you have the two halves made, sew them together, aligning all the points the same as before and making sure that your center seams match. Press the seams open.

Measure your finished blocks. Are they 9½"? If so, great—you are right on the money. Cut 12 – 9½" squares of the large pink print fabric for your alternate blocks. If they are a little larger or smaller consistently, don't fret. You are going to use the YUM (Your Unique Measurement) principle again. If all your blocks measure out to be 9⅝", cut your alternate block squares that size.

To construct the alternate block, you will use the same method you did for making the star sashing in Class 330, page 39 by adding a square to each corner of your large alternate block square and sewing on the diagonal. No matter the size you have to scale your alternate block up or down to, the triangles on the corners are a given size and need to match those on the design block. The triangles on your design blocks should measure 3½". Cut 48 squares this size. You will need 4 strips cut 3½" wide. Once you have your squares cut, mark them lightly with a pencil from corner to corner diagonally in one direction. Place 1 at each corner on your alternate blocks. Sew on your marked line. Once all your corners are sewn on, press the triangles so they complete the corner and starch. Measure ¼" to the right of your stitching line and cut to trim off the extra fabric of both the green and the large pink print.

Now you are ready to assemble your blocks into rows and finish your quilt top.

Again, you will need to use a pin to align where the points of the large pink print triangles of the design blocks meet the points of green triangles on your design blocks—but this is easy after assembling the design blocks!

Quilt layout diagram

CARRIE'S LOG CABIN BASKET

Log Cabin Basket

Quilt top size: 52" × 52"

Grid size: ¾"

Blocks: 25

Layout: 5 rows of 5 blocks

Yardages for quilt top:

⅛ yard each of 5–6 browns, 4–5 peaches, and 4–5 teals

¼ yard each of 7–8 creams

¼ yard of brown multicolored print

½ yard of brown tonal for outer borders

This is a fun little quilt to make and adds another dimension to working with Log Cabin blocks. As you read earlier, the Log Cabin block can be considered a two-bell block, in that is has a definite diagonal line and two different corners—basically it looks like a half-square triangle. That means that for any block design you can create using half-square triangles, you can substitute a Log Cabin block.

We are going to use this principle to make a picture quilt. There are five different Log Cabin blocks to construct in this quilt. These blocks are offset or lopsided blocks, meaning they do not have the same number of logs on each side. The light sides of the two-color blocks only have two logs each, whereas the dark sides have three logs each. This helps to create the "picture" of the basket design in this quilt.

The grid size of the Log Cabin blocks is ¾" finished. We are going to use the exact same piecing techniques we used for the other two log cabin quilts in Volumes 1 and 2. If you remember, we cut the strips slightly larger than needed and trim them down so they are the exact size needed when finished; so we are going to cut the strips 1⅜". As this is an odd size, you may want to use Glow-Line Tape or some other sort of marker to make sure that you line up the proper line of your ruler with the edge of your fabric when you are cutting your strips.

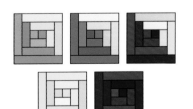

Five different Log Cabin block colorations for Basket quilt

Let's get started cutting! For each 2-color block, you will need to cut 1 strip of each of your fabrics for the teal and peach blocks and 2 strips each of your creams and browns.

Start constructing this quilt by making the single all-brown block and the 10 brown and cream blocks. To start creating your blocks, you will need to decide how scrappy you would like them to look. You can choose a single fabric for your center squares, or you can work with up to 3 fabrics to make them. If you choose a single fabric, you will need a 15" strip of that chosen fabric. If you are using more than 1 fabric, you will need either 7½" or 5" strips for 2- or 3-color centers respectively.

Begin by sewing those center fabric strips onto strips of your other browns.

Again, you need to decide how random and scrappy you want your blocks to turn out. Carrie chose a single brown fabric for her center squares but chose 2 different fabrics for the first logs. She cut the center fabric in half and sewed each half to a strip of 2 different fabrics. There is no right or wrong here.

Once you have your center strips together, press the seam allowance toward the log and then cut your strip(s) so that you have 11 – 1⅜" units. Next, sew those units to another strip or a number of strips of your other brown fabrics, remembering to leave ¼" space between each center unit if you are placing more than 1 unit on a single strip. Cut your units apart if necessary, press the seam allowance again to the log you just sewed on, starch, and trim. Measuring

from each seamline, you need to trim all 3 pieces you have sewn so far down to 1". (Refer to Cabin in the Cotton, Volume 2, Class 240, pages 43–48, if you need detailed instructions for doing this.)

Once you have these units trimmed, it is time to make a color change for 10 of your blocks. Ten of these will now have 2 cream logs added, and 1 block will continue to have browns added. Again, refer to either Patriotic Log Cabin (Volume 1, Class 140, pages 43–46) or Cabin in the Cotton (Volume 2, Class 240, pages 43–48) for specific instructions for sewing, pressing, and trimming your blocks to size.

Remember, this quilt is ending up with ¾" finished logs, so when you trim, make sure they are cut to 1" wide.

Once you have 10 blocks with 2 brown and 2 cream logs added, you will go back to brown and add 2 more logs. Then it is back to cream, adding 2 logs, and for the final round, you will add the last 2 brown logs.

For the all-brown blocks you are making, just keep adding brown logs until you have a total of 10 logs. Refer to the earlier diagram of the block colorations to check that your blocks have the correct color placement and number of logs.

The 9 all-cream blocks are constructed just like the single all-brown block you just made, and the teal and peach blocks will be made the same as the brown and cream blocks. Construct these next.

Ideally, when you have finished all 25 of your blocks and trimmed them, they should measure 5″ square. Yours may be slightly smaller or larger depending on your pressing and the fabrics you have used, but as long as the blocks are of a consistent size, you are now ready to assemble the center of your quilt. If you have a few blocks that are a completely different size from the rest, you may want to take the time to construct replacement blocks, making sure that you pressed well and trimmed each of your logs every time 2 logs were added.

Lay out your Log Cabin blocks according to the quilt photograph. Using the chain sewing techniques we taught you in Volume 1, Class 130 (pages 34–35), assemble the center of your quilt top. Be mindful of which direction you are pressing your seam allowances so that the blocks nest together nicely when you sew the rows together.

Now you need to make the 2 large Log Cabin blocks that you will cut in half to make your on-point center into a square quilt top. To start this process, you need to determine how large you need to make these blocks so that they fit the outside edges of your center. To do this, measure through the center of your assembled basket. You could have ended up with a measurement anywhere from 21¾″ to 24½″. This is okay, as you can accommodate the size of your center by adding logs to your large blocks or taking them away. Carrie's quilt center ended up measuring 23½″. This measurement is what the diagonal measurement of your large Log Cabin block needs to end up being.

For example, 23.5″ ÷ 1.414 = 16.62″—not exactly ruler friendly. Round this number up to 17″ and see what the diagonal measurement ends up being: 17″ × 1.414 = 24.04″ or 24″—that works! So now we need to determine how many logs it will take to make a block that size.

Your logs finish to be ¾″. 17″ ÷ .75″ = 22.66. You need 22 logs and a bit more. What if you made the center of your large block 2″ instead of ¾″? Subtract 2″ from 17″, and you get 15″. Divide that by .75″, and you magically get 20 logs needed—these are nice numbers. So depending on what size your center ended up being, you may need to use a 2″ center, stay with a ¾″ center, or find some other measurement that fits the size of block you need to create.

In the case of the example above, you will need 10 logs on each side of your center square to create a 17″ block. Of these 10 logs, the last 3 logs are cut from the focus fabric you have chosen. Simple subtraction tells you that you need to sew 7 cream logs to each side of the center and then switch to your focus fabric and sew 3 of those to each side.

No matter the size block you end up needing to make, you want the last 3 logs to be the focus fabric. Once you have this determined, construct these 2 large blocks. Press, starch, and trim each round of logs.

Now it's time to cut all your hard work in half. Using a 24″ ruler, line the edge of your ruler up with the diagonal of your block and cut corner to corner, carefully and slowly; you need this edge to be as straight and clean as possible.

Once you have your 4 halves, pin 2 of them to opposite sides of your center block, being careful to align the center of the half Log Cabin block with the center of the center piece. With the half Log Cabin block toward your feed dogs to help control the bias, sew these 2 corners onto your quilt top center. Press toward the half Log Cabin blocks and repeat for the other 2 halves. Once these are attached and pressed, trim your outer logs of focus fabric down to 1″ (if you haven't already). It is now time to add the 3 outer border strips.

Straighten your fabric and cut 12 – 1⅜″ strips of the tonal brown. Just as you added borders for all the quilt tops you made from Volumes 1 and 2, measure your quilt top through the center horizontally and cut 2 of your strips to this length; pin and sew them to the quilt top. Trim them down to 1″. Measure the quilt top through the center from top to bottom. Cut 2 more strips this length; pin and sew. Continue this process until you have added a total of 3 border strips to each side of your quilt.

And that's it—a lot of sewing, but look at the wonderful creation you have to show for all your work! Enjoy!

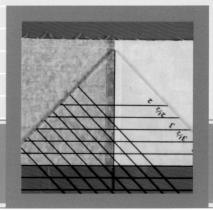

Class 340

LESSON ONE:
Workspace upgrades

In Volume 1, we gave you ideas on how much electricity you need to power everything you might have going on in your workspace effectively. Volume 2 addressed ways to provide sufficient light where you sew. Now it is time to look at the lighting situation in your room and give you a formula to check if you have sufficient light for your sewing area.

Lighting is one item that must not be overlooked in your workspace. Without proper and sufficient light, eye fatigue can constantly plague you. Whether you prefer track, fluorescent, or overhead incandescent lighting, having sufficient wattage is the most important item.

> *note* We are not addressing the green movement here, just providing information. A federal mandate will phase out the use of incandescent bulbs beginning in 2012. This might be something that you want to take into consideration when choosing a lighting type. It would be money well spent to hire a lighting professional to look at your situation and let you know what types of new lighting are available and will fit in with the new laws. At the time of this writing, we are still two years out, so we are encouraging you to take the initiative to see what is available at the time you need the information. This will get you started.

Interior designers use standard formulas to figure the amount of light needed for different activities. These formulas measure light in foot-candles.

A foot-candle is equal to the amount of light a candle throws on an object a foot away.

Accepted light levels for sewing are as follows:

❋ 20–50 foot-candles for occasional machine sewing and high-contrast fabrics

❋ 50–100 foot-candles for machine sewing on light to medium fabrics

❋ 100–200 foot-candles for machine sewing on dark fabrics with low contrast

❋ 100–200 foot-candles for fine hand sewing

❋ 500 foot-candles for sewing black thread on black fabric

A light source or lamp of a given wattage has a light output measured in lumens.

Lumens are a unit of light that will deliver a level of one foot-candle to a surface one foot square at a distance of one foot.

Following is a list of lumen output for various types of lighting:

Lumens per Watt Output

Incandescent	20
Fluorescent	80
Mercury	50
HID (high intensity discharge)	85

It is possible to calculate the level of illumination (in foot-candles) that a fixture and spacing will give. The same formula, in reverse, can suggest the number and spacing of fixtures needed to produce a desired level of illumination.

Illumination (in foot-candles) = lumens supplied (lumens per watt × wattage) ÷ area in square feet to be lighted.

Using the formula, let's work through an example. If a room is 16′ × 20′, we have 320 square feet of space to light. If we choose fluorescent lighting, we will be getting 80 lumens per watt. Fluorescent tubes average 40 watts per tube. Multiply 80 (lumens per watt) by 40 (wattage of a tube) to get 3,200 lumens. Next, 3,200 ÷ 320 square feet = 10 foot-candles supplied. We know from the above chart that we need an average of 50–100 foot-candles for machine sewing. If 10 foot-candles are supplied by 1 fluorescent tube, we will need 5 to 10 tubes to light the room sufficiently.

What if we reverse the formula? We know we need 50–100 foot-candles of illumination for the task. Multiply this by the square footage of the room: 50 × 320 = 16,000 lumens needed. Divide the lumens needed by the lumens per watt output: 16,000 ÷ 80 = 200. This tells you how many watts are needed. Divide this by the wattage given by each tube (40), and you have how many tubes you need: 200 ÷ 40 = 5 to 10 tubes.

What if you plan on track lighting and want to use 60-watt long-life or energy-saving bulbs? Each light bulb will give 1,200 lumens. Divide 1,200 by 320 square feet to get 3.75 foot-candles of illumination. To get sufficient illumination of 50–100 foot-candles, divide 100 (50) by 3.75, which equals 27 (13) light bulbs needed. If using 75-watt bulbs, only 21 (11) are needed. If using 100-watt bulbs, only 16 (8) are needed.

These calculations are easy to figure and will help you check on your present lighting and determine how much additional lighting you may

need to add. If the area is too bright and glaring for sewing, light can be taken away.

When purchasing light bulbs, look for translucent bulbs. Opaque bulbs cannot be seen through, giving mood lighting. Transparent bulbs are see-through and tend to give harsh, glaring light, whereas translucent bulbs are only partially see-through and give a softer light.

When reviewing your lighting requirements and space layout, consider the natural lighting that is available to the space and how you can use it to your advantage. Natural light can be soft and illuminating or bright and glaring. Will you need window coverings to keep out glare or ones that can be opened fully during the day and closed at night for privacy and light retention?

Consider how you're storing your fabrics when choosing lighting fixtures. Incandescent bulbs can give off a yellow tint to colors but will not cause any fading. Fluorescent tubes are available in several types, including full spectrum, which will keep colors true.

Fluorescent tubes have been reported to cause fading, but filters can be installed that will decrease the possibility of this happening. Track lighting can be directed to the areas you want lighted, but if sufficient wattage is not supplied, it will be spotty and create shadows in the room. Halogen lighting gets very warm, becoming uncomfortable on warm days or in a small space. There are many decisions to make, and we hope this helps you get started in your search for the perfect light for you!

Quarter-square triangles (hourglass squares)

Quarter-square triangle squares have many design applications. They can be two, three, or four different colors in one square. They are often used as connector blocks, and many blocks use them within their design elements.

Quarter-square triangle

The basis of this unit is one-quarter of a square. If you wanted to rotary cut the individual units or use templates, you would need to know how much seam allowance is added to the square in order to accommodate the triangles. Looking at the triangle below, you will see that 1¼″ needs to be added to the finished size of the triangle in order to add seam allowances.

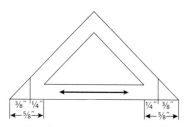

Quarter-square triangle

As an example, let's work with a 3″ grid: 1¼″ added to 3″ = 4¼″ square needed. Cut a square 4¼″ and then cut it in half diagonally twice. The long side of the triangle is straight grain. Use a template or corner-trimming ruler to trim the points for easier and more accurate piecing.

You always add 1¼" to the finished size for seam allowances on quarter-square triangles or "cut-to-size" piecing.

Traditionally, these squares are made by sewing pairs of these small triangles together, pressing, and then joining the pairs. What you now know about sewing on the bias edge and sewing small triangles will tell you that this method would be iffy for accuracy. There is a quicker and more accurate way to construct quarter-square triangles.

Instead of cutting individual units, you will start with half-square triangles. If you cut a half-square triangle in half diagonally across the seam, you have two halves that are a mirror image. Each half is one-half of a quarter-square triangle.

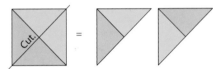

Half-square triangle cut in half to get mirror-image quarter-square triangles

To get the color placement correct, cut another half-square triangle in half. You will see that you can now place the colors opposite each other so that the block is now a true quarter-square triangle—in fact, you get two identical units.

Two quarter-square triangle units from two half squares

For a sample, we will work with the Sew and Slice method from Class 310, Lesson Four (page 14), to construct the quarter-square triangle units. Start out making half-square triangle units (adding 1¼"–1½" to the finished size

[3"] for seam allowance) in any color combination of your choice (see note).

> **note** You can use any method you learned in Classes 310 and 320 to construct the half-square triangles. If you need them very scrappy, making only a few of each color combination is good, so the methods in Class 310 might suit your needs. If you need many of the same colors together, any of the techniques in Class 320—Sheeting, Bias strips, Eight from a square, and Triangle paper—are all good methods. Quarter-square triangle paper is available in a few sizes. Here we walk you through making just a few units, but that is only for learning purposes to make a few samples. We strongly suggest that you make these half-square triangle units using a 1½" seam allowance allotment so there is room for trimming.

Once you construct the original half-square triangle squares, press to set the seam, starch, and press again on the right side to get a sharp crease on the seam. *This time we do not cut the squares in half.* Turn half of the squares over to the wrong side and draw a line from corner to corner diagonally across (perpendicular to) the first seam.

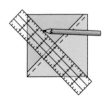

Draw line perpendicular to seam.

Pair up two half-square triangle squares, keeping the one with the

drawn line on the top, right sides together. Check that you have opposite fabrics on top of one another, light on dark and dark on light. Butt (nest) the seams together tightly. Pin the squares together to keep the seams tight to one another. Start sewing on the left side of the line, using whatever guide you have established for guiding off a line. Chain sew all the pairs. Turn at the end and sew along the left side of the line again.

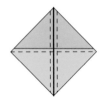

Sewing on both sides of line

> **tip** If you need very scrappy quarter-square triangles for a particular quilt, make a variety of half-square triangle squares using many different fabrics. Once they are cut and pressed, mix them up so that you get as many combinations as possible.

Press to set the seam and then cut the squares on the line. You now have two identical quarter-square triangle units. Press the seam. (These seam intersections can be fanned, as learned in Volume 1, Class 150, Lesson Six, page 58.)

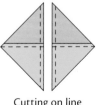

Cutting on line

We find that the best ruler for trimming these pieces is Marsha McCloskey's Precision Trimmer 6.

This ruler has plenty of lines—especially the diagonals—that allow you to double-check that everything is straight and square before you cut. Trim each unit to 3½".

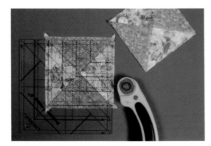

Trimming with Precision Trimmer 6

LESSON THREE:
Three-piece triangle squares

We have three different methods for you to try for these units. They have their pluses, and once you make your samples, you will be able to choose which one will give you the accuracy you need for your project.

Three-piece triangle square

When you start looking at individual quilt blocks to see what makes the design develop, you will eventually find an interesting unit that is made up of two small triangles and one large one. The one thing you have to consider with any pattern using this unit is whether all the three-piece triangle units are identical or some of them are a mirror image of each other. If you start making the unit in the same manner as the quarter-square triangles above were made, you will wind up with mirror-image blocks. If you need them to all be the same, the original two squares for

quarter-square triangles will need to be sewn a bit differently.

Here are three different methods to make these units.

METHOD ONE

This block starts out using squares similar to those used in making quarter-square triangles. The squares are cut 1½" larger than the finished unit you need. This allows for a bit of fudge room and trimming.

Let's start by making mirror-image three-piece triangle squares. Start by cutting two squares, 1½" larger than the finished size you need, from the fabrics that you are using for the two small triangles. Pair them right sides together and draw a line from corner to corner diagonally, in one direction only. Stitch on both sides of the line. Press and cut apart diagonally on the line. You now have two half-square triangle squares. Press the seam allowance toward the dark triangle.

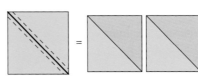

Two half-square units

Cut squares 1¼" larger than the finished size from the fabric that represents the large triangle. These squares will be the same size as the triangle squares you just constructed. With right sides together, place one half-square triangle unit on top of the solid square. Draw a line diagonally, corner to corner, perpendicular to the seam. Stitch on both sides of this line.

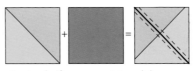

Sewing half-square unit to solid square

Press and then cut corner to corner on the drawn line. When you open the units, you will see that they are a mirror image of each other. Using the Precision Trimmer 6, align all the seams to the ruler lines and trim them to the exact unfinished size, making sure that the seams are exactly in the corners.

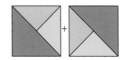

Three-piece triangle squares that are mirror images of one another

METHOD TWO

If your pattern calls for all the units to be the same, not mirror imaged, there is a clever way to get around that problem. The light and dark squares are cut 1½" larger than the desired finished square. Draw a line from corner to corner along both diagonals on the wrong side of the lightest fabric square. Now, refer to the photos below to choose which side of the unit you need the dark triangle to be positioned on.

If you want the dark triangle to be on the left side when the unit is sewn and pressed open, stitch on the left side of each drawn line, changing sides at the center point of the intersecting drawn lines.

Dark triangle on left side

If you want the dark triangles to be on the right, stitch on the right side of each line.

Dark triangle on right side

Once all four lines are stitched, cut the square apart on both drawn diagonal lines. Press and lightly starch the seam allowances toward the dark triangle.

Unlike the mirror-image blocks, these blocks have to be constructed by cutting large triangles and sewing on the bias edge. This is one technique where we strongly recommend that the method you choose for making the original small triangles is not mathematically correct measurements. Having the ability to square up the finished unit to size ensures that the corners are accurate, resulting in perfect points when you sew the units together into larger blocks.

Using the Precision Trimmer 6, align all the lines of the ruler with the seamlines, centering to the cut size you need. Trim all four sides, making sure that the seams are exactly in the corners. You now have four identical three-piece triangle blocks.

Results = four identical units

METHOD THREE

Do you remember the Wonder Cut Ruler in Class 320, Lesson Three, page 22? If you found the ruler and tried it, you probably think it is pretty slick, especially if you don't like to remember the formulas for sizes. This ruler gives you a fun way of making three-piece triangle units using the ruler. All of the three-piece triangle squares are oriented the same; you do not have to switch sides for sewing with this method as you do in Method Two to get them all the same.

Begin by selecting your three fabrics. You will need to determine which fabrics will make up the large triangle. The other two fabrics will each be a small triangle on the other side of the square.

Before you start, remember that the ruler instructions ask for on-grain fabric, which will result in bias edges on the finished square. You have a choice of working with bias strips in the construction phase to get on-grain squares, or with on-grain fabric strips for construction, resulting in bias edges on your squares. Not everyone minds working with bias, and with enough starch it is not a huge problem, so try both and make your own decision.

Start by cutting strips for the large triangle. For our example, we are going to make 4″ finished units. Cut using the 4½″ line.

 tip If you are cutting bias strips, you will find that this ruler is not long enough to get from edge to edge of your fabric. We suggest that you use your favorite rotary ruler and measure from the edge of the ruler that says "cut along this edge" to each of the lines. Make a note of what that actual measurement is. When your fabric is too long for your Wonder Cut Ruler, cut the strips with your longer rotary ruler using the measurement you just noted.

Next, cut the remaining two fabrics using the 4½″ line. Stitch these two fabrics together on one long side with your scant ¼″ seam allowance. Press the seams open.

Cut this strip set into 4½″ segments.

Sew these units end to end into a long strip. Each color will alternate.

New strip of squares

Place this new strip on top of the first strip (the large triangle fabric), right sides together. Check that both strips are exactly the same width. If they're not, trim them to be exactly the measurement on the Wonder Cut Ruler. Sew ¼″ seams down both long sides.

Align the corner triangle area of the Wonder Cut Ruler with the bottom edge on the fabric, using the same number you used to cut the strips (in this example 4½"). Be sure that the center marked line in the corner of the ruler aligns exactly with the seams of the pieced strip. Cut both sides of the corner.

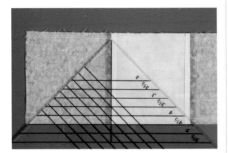

Ruler placement

Slide the ruler down and align the ruler line with the third seam. Cut. There is a unit between the two cuts that is automatically cut to size.

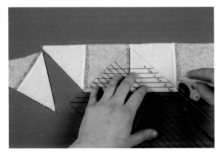

Slide ruler down to third seam.

Press, starch, and trim if necessary for accuracy.

note We find these to be very accurate, but only if everything is spot-on through the complete process. Because there is no fudge room for trimming, any inaccuracy is not fixable once the pieces are cut.

The quilts
PRAIRIE WINDMILLS

Prairie Windmills quilt

Quilt top size: 56" × 56" without borders

Grid size: 4"

Blocks: 49

Layout: 7 rows of 7 blocks

Yardages for quilt top:

2 yards light yellow

1¼ yards dark yellow

1¼ yards white (does not include borders)

This quilt is made up entirely of identical three-piece triangle units—no mirror-image units are used. You will need to use the instructions for having the dark small triangle on the right side of the unit, using Method Two on page 57.

Each Windmill block is made up of 4 of the three-piece triangle units.

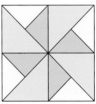

Windmill block

You will be constructing 49 of the above block. Each unit has 1 pair of small triangles, and you will get 4 of these units from each square you cut. Therefore, you will need 49 squares of the 2 fabrics that create the 2 small triangles.

Cut:

7 – 5½" strips dark yellow

7 – 5½" strips white

You can get 7 – 5½" squares from each strip. Cut 49 – 5½" squares of both dark yellow and white.

Place a dark yellow and a white square right sides together. Repeat this for all 49 squares of each color. Draw diagonal lines corner to corner, in both directions, on the white squares. Draw a line ¼" away from these lines, staying on the right side of each half of the line. The line will change sides at the center intersection.

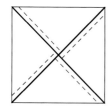

Dark triangle on right side

Stitch on the short lines, changing sides at the center intersection. Press the square and then cut corner to corner on the diagonal lines, in both directions. Press the seam allowances toward the dark yellow triangle. You will have 196 triangle units.

These units will be sewn to larger triangles. The larger triangles come from squares cut ¼" smaller than the squares cut for the small triangle units. Four triangles are needed for each block, and you will get 2 triangles per square. Be sure to starch the fabric before you cut the strips. The strips will be cut into squares that are then cut into triangles. Starch will help stabilize the fabric when sewing the bias edges.

You will need to cut 13 – 5¼" strips of light yellow, subcut into 98 – 5¼" squares.

Pair together 1 large light yellow triangle and 1 unit of 2 small triangles. Carefully align the long side

and stitch. This edge is bias, so feed the pieces into the machine carefully. As you sew, make sure that you keep the points at the end of the seam straight and do not let the seam allowance vary as you stitch off the edge. Continue pairing the 2 units and chain sew all the units together. Starch the light yellow squares before cutting them in half to help eliminate some stretching problems.

Press the seam allowance toward the large light yellow triangle. Starch lightly. Using the Precision Trimmer 6, square the pressed units to measure exactly 4½". Again, check that all seams are precisely in the corners.

Now that all 196 units are constructed and trimmed, lay out 4 of them to form the Windmill block. You can streamline the sewing by making stacks of 49 units in the 4 positions that make the block.

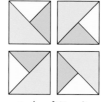

Four stacks of 49 units each

Start by sewing the 2 units of Row 1. Place the top unit on the right stack on top of the top unit on the left stack. Once you align the right edges, you will see that the seams that nest together are at the end of the seam. You will have much more success in getting the points perfect at this intersection if you flip the pair over and start stitching at the edge where all the seams come together. If you don't do this, the presser foot can push the seams out of alignment, and you will not get the 4 points to form exactly.

Check the intersecting seams to make sure they are nested exactly to form the first points. Press the seam allowance toward the large triangle. Lightly starch the seam, being very careful not to stretch and distort the block while using the iron.

Now you have joined pairs. Lay out the block again into the 2 rows and start to join them together. This time you have 8 points coming together at the center of the seam. There is a lot of thickness here, so sew slowly and aim for the intersection where all the threads cross. It is most helpful to open the 2 units and visually place the intersecting points into position and then sew.

Once it is sewn, open the block and examine the points. They all need to come together exactly. If they don't, check to see if one of the nested seams is a bit off. This is the most common problem for matching points. You will start to discover that anytime the original 2 pieces were sewn together and the points did not come together exactly, this problem always results. If you don't start with exact points, you can't end up with exact points. Don't "save time" by not correcting these small problems when they first occur—you will only pay for it in the end. This will be driven home when we start working with eight-pointed stars in Volume 4.

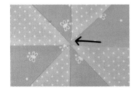

Points that don't come together because of seams that didn't nest properly

Fan the center intersection of this seam and press. By fanning the seams, you distribute the bulk of the seam allowance; this will make it easier to press and quilt.

Continue with these techniques to sew the blocks together, and then the rows together.

Once the quilt top is finished, measure all 4 sides to ensure that they are all the same length and width before adding the borders of your choice. If needed, review the instructions for preparing and adding borders in Volume 1, Class 180, page 93.

Yankee Puzzle

Quilt top size: 56″ × 56″

Grid size: 4″

Blocks:

25 Yankee Puzzle blocks (100 hour-glass squares)

24 alternate blocks

Layout: 7 rows of 7 blocks

Yardages for quilt top:

A total of 1¼ yards of 3 light, 3 medium, and 3 dark blues

1¼ yards of background for the quarter-square triangles

1½ yards of light shirting for the alternate blocks

Following is an illustration of a block. Each pieced block in the quilt is an 8″ square finished and contains 4 quarter-square triangle units. Each 8″ block uses 8 assorted blue triangles and 8 light triangles.

Yankee Puzzle

Using the technique used earlier in Lesson Two, start by determining what size squares you need for the first process. If we have a 4″ grid, you need to add 1½″ to 4″ to get 5½″ squares to start with. We are using a variety of blue fabrics and 1 white for the quarter-square triangle units. Determine how many units of each fabric you want and figure how many squares you need to cut for your color choices. For our quilt, we made the quarter-square units very scrappy. We paired different blues in each quarter-square triangle unit, and different units to make up each block. Cut the following number of squares of each of your blues for the quilt shown:

4 – 5½" light blue #1 squares

6 – 5½" light blue #2 squares

6 – 5½" light blue #3 squares

6 – 5½" medium blue #1 squares

5 – 5½" medium blue #2 squares

6 – 5½" medium blue #3 squares

6 – 5½" dark blue #1 squares

6 – 5½" dark blue #2 squares

5 – 5½" dark blue #3 squares

50 – 5½" white #1 squares

24 – 8½" white #2 squares (alternate block)

Pair up a blue square with a white square. Once you have 50 pairs, draw a line corner to corner on each white square. Chain sewing, sew on both sides of the line, ¼" from the line. Press to set the seam. Cut on the line and press the seam allowance toward the blue triangle.

Process of making quarter-square triangle units

Once you have all the half-square pieces pressed, mix and match any combinations you want the blues to be in—light/light, light/medium, medium/medium, light/dark, medium/dark, dark/dark, and so forth. Try to make as many variations as you can.

Make a mix of blue combinations.

Align the seam to butt tightly. Draw a line perpendicular to the seam. Stitch ¼" on both sides of the line, chain sewing for efficiency. Once all the squares are sewn, separate the chain and press to set the seams.

Sewing second line

You will now get 2 quarter-square units for each cut. As you cut on the line, open the unit and check that the intersections are nested tightly and butted accurately. If some aren't, now is the time to take the stitches out and try again. Be careful this time, as you are working on a bias-cut edge.

Two units

Trim all the squares to exactly 4½". Again, we suggest that you use the Precision Trimmer 6 so that you can use both diagonal lines to check on the corners. Once the ruler is aligned with the corners and the center intersection, place the index finger of the ruler hand on the corner of the ruler to prevent slippage. Cut all 4 sides to get perfect squares.

Take all the quarter-square triangle squares to your design wall or floor and start to lay them out so you get a good variation and mix of the values of blue. Position the squares so that the white triangle is next to a blue triangle—the squares alternate or turn a quarter turn next to each other. Add the alternate blocks and make any changes you feel necessary in the color placement. See the photo on page 61.

Four quarter-square units sewn together to make a block

Stitch the 4 quarter-square triangle units together, being very careful that all the points line up at the edges as well as at the center seam. This is truly where the trimming pays huge dividends! Press carefully. Once the 25 blocks are constructed, sew the blocks into rows and sew the rows together.

tip If you are consistently having problems with your points, go back and check your trimming. We find that different rulers have different line widths and thicknesses, and often the line is not *exactly* in the corner of the ruler. Between the ruler line being thick and hard to see if it is exactly on the seamline, and the line not being exactly on in the corner, your chances of trimming accurately are slim. One of the reasons we strongly recommend the Precision Trimmer 6 is the lines are thin and printed exactly in the corners. Your workmanship is only as good as the tools you are working with.

No doubt you are noticing how much more time these quilts take than the quilts we covered in Volumes 1 and 2. There are more things to look for, and precision and accuracy are starting to be of priority. Things you can get away with on simpler quilts are very obvious on anything with triangles. If you are having any problems with these quilts, go back and again check the accuracy of the cutting, seam allowance, pressing, and trimming, and really pay attention to the placement of the trimming ruler when trimming seam allowances. We can't stress enough the importance of trimming and having the seam exactly in the point of the corner. If it isn't, your chances of having precise points are pretty slim. Again, slow down and take your time. These quilts are very stunning, and when they are pieced right on, they are quite impressive.

Class 350

LESSON ONE:

Drafting blocks with triangles

In Volumes 1 and 2 of this series, we covered basic drafting and explained base grids and changing block sizes using this process. We covered simple Four-Patch and Nine-Patch blocks in the previous books, and now we are ready to explore blocks that have other shapes, such as triangles and rectangles.

Once you have selected a block pattern and assigned a base grid to it, you can identify the various pattern pieces needed. It's helpful to draw a diagram of the shapes, rather than taking the time to write out all the words. (Draw a square instead of writing out *square*.) Then once you have assigned the size to the various pattern pieces, indicate that size on the pattern piece diagrams for easy reference later. Below are a few of the common shapes and symbols:

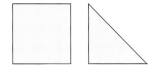

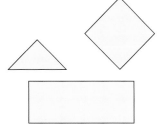

Square, half-square triangle, quarter-square triangle, square on point, rectangle

Be consistent when labeling the symbols so that you can easily interpret what you wrote. For a square, determine the size of the square (finished size) and write this measurement at the left of the symbol, as shown.

2″ square

A half-square triangle is literally half of a square. For this kind of triangle, the side measurement is also placed at the left of the symbol; this is the one measurement you can determine.

2″ half-square triangle

A quarter-square triangle is one-fourth of a square, as shown. The measurement should be noted under the base of the triangle because the base is the measurement that can be determined.

2″ quarter-square triangle

A rectangle requires two size notations, since there are two different side measurements. Place the numbers as indicated on the following diagram.

1″ × 2″ rectangle

Another shape you'll encounter is a square on point. For this shape, write the measurement inside the symbol with small dashes pointing toward the four corners, as shown, since this is what we know about this shape.

4″ square on point

Draw a diagram of any other shapes you encounter in a block and label the measurements as you determine them. Don't worry about knowing the actual mathematical name of these shapes. It really doesn't matter what you call the shape, as long as the diagram you draw has correct measurements.

Let's look at some other traditional patchwork blocks to see if we can determine the pattern pieces needed and their finished sizes.

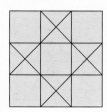

Base grid is a 9-patch with three equal divisions (units).

2″ per unit = 3 × 2″ = 6″ finished block
Pattern pieces needed are 2″ □ △2″

3″ per unit = 3 × 3″ = 9″ finished block
Pattern pieces needed are 3″ □ △3″

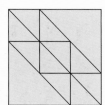

Base grid is a 9-patch with three equal divisions (units).

2″ per unit = 3 × 2″ = 6″ finished block
Pattern pieces needed are 2″ ◺ 4″ ◺

3″ per unit = 3 × 3″ = 9″ finished block
Pattern pieces needed are 3″ ◺ 6″ ◺

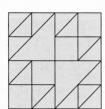

Base grid is a 4-patch with four equal divisions (units).

2″ per unit = 4 × 2″ = 8″ finished block
Pattern pieces needed are 2″ ◺ 4″ ◺ 2″ □

3″ per unit = 4 × 3″ = 12″ finished block
Pattern pieces needed are 3″ ◺ 6″ ◺ 3″ □

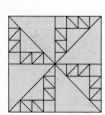

Base grid is a 4-patch with eight equal divisions (units).

1″ per unit = 8 × 1″ = 8″ finished block
Pattern pieces needed are 1″ ◺ 1″ □ 4″ ◺ 2″ ◺

1½″ per unit = 8 × 1½″ = 12″ finished block
Pattern pieces needed are 1½″ ◺ 1½″ □ 6″ ◺ 3″ ◺

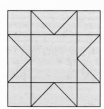

Base grid is a 4-patch with four equal divisions (units).

1½″ per unit = 4 × 1½″ = 6″ finished block
Pattern pieces needed are 1½″ ◺ 1½″ □ △3″ 3″ □

2″ per unit = 4 × 2″ = 8″ finished block
Pattern pieces needed are 2″ ◺ 2″ □ △4″ 4″ □

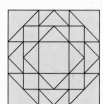

Base grid is a 9-patch with six equal divisions (units).

1½″ per unit = 6 × 1½″ = 9″ finished block
Pattern pieces needed are 1½″ ◺ 3″ ◺ △3″ 3″ □ 1½″ □

2″ per unit = 6 × 2″ = 12″ finished block
Pattern pieces needed are 2″ ◺ 4″ ◺ △4″ 4″ □ 2″ □

The true basics of drafting any block can be summed up by:

✳ Determining the base grid of the block

✳ Determining the finished size you want the block to be

✳ Determining the number of pattern pieces needed

✳ Determining the finished size of each pattern piece needed

Many quilters work with templates to create the shapes and sizes of each pattern piece to cut around. The seam allowance is added to the template and eliminates the need to remember the measurements. If you choose to rotary cut everything, *always remember to take the finished pattern numbers and convert them into numbers that reflect the addition of seam allowances so they can be rotary cut without templates.* There are times that it is not worth the math computations, making templates much easier to deal with. You might find that you will use a combination of both templates and rotary cutting for some projects.

We will first look at the conversion of finished numbers to cutting numbers when working without templates. Below are the numbers for the basic shapes where the math involved is relatively simple.

Squares = finished size + ½".

2″   2½″

Finished square = cut square

Rectangles = finished size + ½" both directions.

1″   1½″

2″   2½″

Finished rectangle = cut rectangle

Half-square triangles = finished size of the side plus ⅞"; cut a square and slice once diagonally, corner to corner.

2⅞″   →   →   2″

2″ finished half-square triangle = 2⅞″ square; slice once corner to corner

Quarter-square triangles = finished size of the base plus 1¼"; cut a square and slice twice diagonally, corner to corner.

3¼″   →   →   2″

2″ finished quarter-square triangle = 3¼″ square; slice twice corner to corner

Let's work through drafting a block with various shaped pieces. This block is called Old Maid's Puzzle.

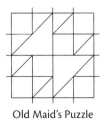

Old Maid's Puzzle

1. Look at the heavy lines in the block illustration and determine what the base grid is. Old Maid's Puzzle is a four-patch with a 4 × 4 grid.

2. Decide on the size of the block you want to make. We will be drafting an 8″ block. This block could easily be made in any size that is divisible by 4—4″, 6″, 8″, 10″, or 12″.

3. Draw an 8″ square on 4-to-the-inch graph paper, using 32 squares by 32 squares. When drawing with a ruler on graph paper, you want to keep the pencil lines exactly on the graph paper lines. Position the edge of the ruler slightly away from the line you are drawing. This allows for the width of the pencil lead. If you are using a desk lamp in your work area, have it on the pencil side of the ruler. This eliminates shadows from the ruler edge.

4. Draw the base grid inside your 8″ square. Remember that the grid dimension is the measurement or size of each division of the square. In this example, we are drafting an 8″ Old Maid's Puzzle that is a four-patch (4 × 4). To determine the grid dimension, divide the size of the block (8″) by the number of equal divisions (4): 8 ÷ 4 divisions = 2″ grid dimension. (Each grid on the paper will represent 2″.) Before drawing in the base grid, be sure to study the block first. You will see that the lines do not go through the large triangle. Omit drawing the lines where they are not needed.

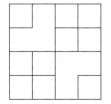

Drawing grid on graph paper

5. Referring to your image of the block you that are drafting, draw in the block design by subdividing the grid. As you draft more and more patterns, you will start to discover that not all grid lines become seamlines. These areas represent grids that are combined and cut as one piece, which we call combined grids.

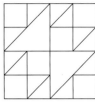

Draw in subdivisions.

6. Identify the shapes needed to cut and sew the block. Draw in the grainlines, making sure the straight grain is on the outside edges of the pieces. In Old Maid's Puzzle, there are 2 shapes—a square and right-angle triangles. There are 2 sizes of triangles. Label the square A, the small triangle B, and the large triangle C.

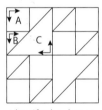

Identify the shapes.

7. Once you identify the shapes, you will need to determine the cutting dimensions of each shape. This is done by adding ¼″ seam allowance to all sides and then measuring the shape. This is simple for the square, as it is a 2″ grid. Add ¼″ to all sides, and you have a 2½″ square. This is easy to cut with a rotary cutter and ruler.

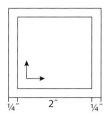

Square with seam allowances added

8. The small triangle B is a 2″ half-square triangle finished. If you want to cut a square in half that will give you 2 triangle shapes that include ¼″ seam allowance on all 3 sides, simply measure that triangle shape from corner to tip, after you have added the seam allowance. Cut your square that size and then cut diagonally.

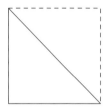

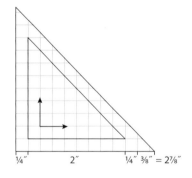

HALF-SQUARE TRIANGLE

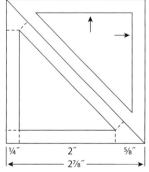

Breakdown of half-square triangle and seam allowance

9. This same method is true when working with a quarter-square triangle. Measure the long side of the quarter-square triangle of the 9″ Ohio Star block below. It is a 3 × 3 grid, so each unit would measure 3″. That would make the long side of the triangle 3″. Add ¼″ seam allowance on all 3 sides, and you will find that the square you need to cut is the finished size (3″) plus 1¼″, or 4¼″ square. Cut this square into quarters diagonally.

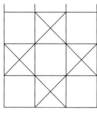

Ohio Star block

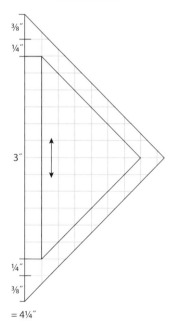

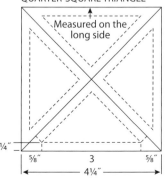

QUARTER-SQUARE TRIANGLE

Breakdown of triangle and seam allowance

CREATING PATTERN PIECES FOR TEMPLATES

There will be times when you design and draft a pattern that will need templates for accuracy. There are numerous ways to make standard-sized shapes, but if the sizes and measurements get wacky, it is much easier to work with templates than fight with a rotary ruler and try to adjust constantly. Flying Geese units are an example of a shape that can be any size, and even many different proportions. These are used as inner components for many block patterns. If the sizes are not standard, templates will help alleviate potential problems.

Here is where you need accurate graph paper. The graph paper grid you select is dependent on the size pattern piece you need to draw. The standard is 4-to-the-inch graph paper,

but if you need a 2⅔" square, you'll need graph paper that can accommodate creating that size. Six-to-the-inch graph paper is not easy to find but is what you need to create a 2⅔" pattern piece. We suggest that you purchase the packet we have made available for working through these books. (See Resources, page 128.)

You always want to draw the finished size of the pattern piece first and then draw around the shape to add the ¼" seam allowance. Having both sets of lines will serve as a constant reminder that the template is complete with seam allowance. Always label the pattern piece with its finished size so you don't accidentally pick up the wrong template.

DRAWING SHAPES ON GRAPH PAPER

To create a square or rectangle, follow the lines of the graph paper and draw the size you need, as shown.

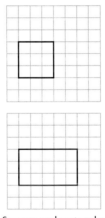

Squares and rectangles

In a half-square triangle, the perpendicular sides are of equal length. Draw the perpendicular sides on the graph paper lines and then draw the diagonal line on the third side, by connecting the end points, as shown.

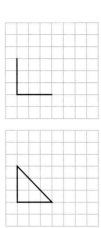

Half-square triangles

With a quarter-square triangle, you need to know the baseline measurement. Begin by drawing the baseline on graph paper.

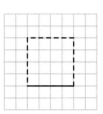

Quarter-square triangle

Mark the midpoint of the baseline. To find the top point of the triangle, measure up from the midpoint the same distance as from the midpoint to the end of the baseline. Mark this point with a dot.

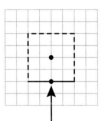

Midpoint of baseline

Connect it to each end of the baseline, as shown, to complete the triangle.

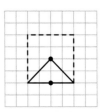

Connect the lines.

To draft a square on point, picture it fitting into a second square where the lines do follow graph paper lines. If the distance tip to tip is 4″, you can draw a 4″ square on the graph paper. Mark the midpoints of each side of the original square.

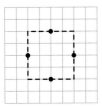

Square on point

Connect the dots, and what you now have is the square on point. Erase the outside 4″ square, and you're set. That was easy enough!

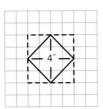

Connect the dots.

ADDING SEAM ALLOWANCES

Seam allowances are added after drawing the finished-size pattern piece. If your graph paper has 4 or 8 squares per inch, the grid lines on the paper can be followed when adding seam allowances to horizontal and vertical pattern lines. Add these seam allowances first, as shown.

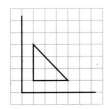

Adding seam allowances

If the number of squares on the paper is not 4 or 8 per inch, or if the seam allowances do not fall on grid lines, you will need to use a ruler to add seam allowances. First, lay the ruler over the pattern piece so that the ¼″ ruler line exactly matches one of the finished lines on the pattern piece. Then back the ruler up just enough to allow for the width of the pencil line and draw as shown.

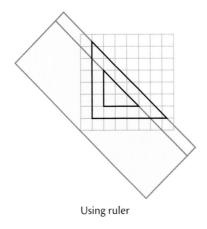

Using ruler

tip We suggest that you do not use a rotary ruler when drafting and adding seam allowances. The C-Thru ruler is the best ruler for this task. You will notice the ⅛″ line on either side of the ruler is each a different measurement. Because these are drafting rulers, the side with the narrowest line is to be used when drawing lines. The line is narrower so that the lead width is accommodated. The opposite side is for measuring.

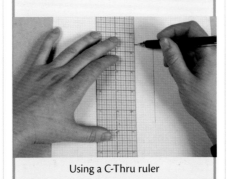

Using a C-Thru ruler

TURNING PATTERN PIECES INTO TEMPLATES

A pattern piece is the shape drawn on graph paper. A template is a sturdy, durable shape that can be used with the rotary cutter to cut fabric. Our goal is to be able to use these templates with rotary cutters for expediency and accuracy.

A common way to make templates is to make a template sandwich with heavyweight template plastic and sandpaper. Glue template plastic on the top side of the graph paper. Glue the sandpaper, rough side out, to the underside of the graph paper. Allow the three layers to dry before cutting out the template. This method is only going to be as successful as the weight of the template plastic and sandpaper. You need them to be quite stiff but light enough to allow you to cut through the layers with scissors. If your materials are too flimsy, you may find that you slice them with your rotary cutter.

Making templates

FLYING GEESE

We will be taking you through four different methods of constructing Flying Geese units in the following lessons. You will find that, as with the half-square triangles, there is a place for each technique. If you want just a few geese to be units in individual blocks or you need really scrappy geese, the first method of making one at a time works well. If you need multiples of the same colorway, the second and third methods are handy. If you need long rows of geese, either color controlled or scrappy, the paper-pieced method is very efficient. No matter which method you are doing, Flying Geese are fun to make and fun to look at in quilts. Enjoy them!

The *Cat Tracks and Bird Trails* quilt is made from the units created by working through each of the techniques. If you make eighteen geese from each technique, you will have enough to construct the quilt top. We strongly suggest that you try each of the methods so you can experience the pros and cons of each and discover which ones are accurate for you. Making samples of each method is one of the best ways to learn what works for you and what doesn't.

LESSON TWO:
Making Flying Geese with folded corners

This method of making Flying Geese blocks is the method most commonly seen in magazines and books. It uses strips cut into rectangles for the geese and squares for the background triangles. It is referred to as stitch and flip corners. The positive aspect is that it is easy to figure the sizes needed for the squares and rectangles, and it is an easy sewing process. You get one goose unit at a time. The drawback is that it requires extreme accuracy to sew on the line or fold exactly; press the corner over; and retain an exact shape, size, and perfect points. We feel that what you save in time, you often give up in accuracy. Make a few of these blocks using this method and see if your finished blocks are exact and the corners give you perfect points.

We are going to make 18 finished 2" × 4" Flying Geese units. You will need 18 rectangles of background (goose) fabric cut 2½" × 4½". You will need 36 squares cut 2½" square for the small (background) triangles.

Prepare the squares by either folding in half exactly and pressing a firm fold or drawing a line diagonally from corner to corner with a mechanical pencil. You can also try to sew corner to corner without a line. Some sewers can eyeball the diagonal of the square while sewing corner to corner. For the rest of us, we tend to need the line of the fold to follow.

Harriet's secret to sewing a straight line is to put the needle in one corner, move your eyes to the opposite corner, and only look at the corner you want to arrive at. Do not look up at the foot or ahead of the foot—just look at the corner, and you will sew an exact straight line. This is the secret to grid quilting perfect straight lines also.

Another way to sew corner to corner accurately is to use a tape guide on the bed of the sewing machine. This allows you to line up the corner of the square during sewing. To create this tape guide, raise the presser foot and lower the needle. Position the ruler up to the edge of the needle, as shown.

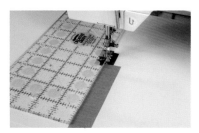

Place tape along edge of ruler.

Drop the presser foot to hold the ruler in place. Take a piece of ¼″ masking tape and position it at the edge of the ruler—up to, but not interfering with, the feed dogs of the machine. Place the strip of tape approximately 3″ toward yourself. Now when you sew corner to corner on the square, you'll line up the corner of the square with the left edge of the tape. Keep the corner of the square along the left edge of the tape and sew. This works because the left edge of the tape is in direct line with the needle.

Line up corner of square with left edge of tape.

We have discussed The Angler 2 earlier as a good tool to assist you in sewing straight seams.

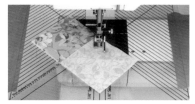

Using The Angler 2

We suggest that you make a sample unit using each of the above methods to see which is most accurate for you, and then proceed to make the eighteen units needed for the quilt top.

CONSTRUCTING THE EIGHTEEN FLYING GEESE BLOCKS

1. Position a small square at the end of the rectangle, right sides together, and sew diagonally, as illustrated. Fold the square toward the corner and press. After pressing, open the square and trim the corner to a ¼″ seam allowance. Re-press.

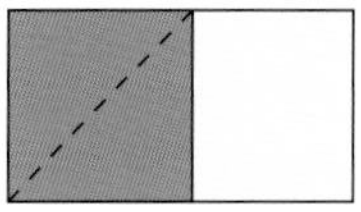

Position square at   Open small triangle.
end of rectangle.

2. On the opposite end of the rectangle, position another small square. Be sure the fold or line is pointing to the top center of the rectangle. Sew carefully toward the opposite corner. Press, open to trim the seam allowance, and press again.

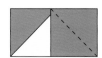

Position and sew second corner.

3. Once the corners are sewn and pressed, measure the rectangle. The bottom points should be exactly in the corner, and the top point needs to be ¼″ from the raw edge. If all this is accurate and the rectangle measures exactly 2½″ × 4½″, you have successfully constructed your Flying Geese units with folded corners.

LESSON THREE:
4X Flying Geese

This method gives you four geese at once. Accuracy in cutting and sewing is a must for this technique, so take your time and sew very straight.

note *A handy ruler named the Flying Geese x4 No Math Ruler (by Lazy Girl Designs) is available that has the size of the squares needed for the technique printed on it. This would eliminate your needing to have the following chart to find out what sizes to cut for different sizes of geese. It is all printed on the ruler.*

Size chart for 4x Flying Geese

Each set of 4 pieced units requires 1 large (A) square and 4 small (B) squares. Cut the size indicated on the chart below for the finished size you need.

Finished size	Large square A goose fabric	Small squares B background fabric
¾″ × 1½″	2¾″	1⅝″
1″ × 2″	3¼″	1⅞″
1¼″ × 2½″	3¾″	2⅛″
1½″ × 3″	4¼″	2⅜″
1¾″ × 3½″	4¾″	2⅝″
2″ × 4″	5¼″	2⅞″
2¼″ × 4½″	5¾″	3⅛″
2½″ × 5″	6¼″	3⅜″
2¾″ × 5½″	6¾″	3⅝″
3″ × 6″	7¼″	3⅞″
3¼″ × 6½″	7¾″	4⅛″
3½″ × 7″	8¼″	4⅜″

With right sides together, align a small square onto one corner of a large square. Position a second square onto the opposite corner (diagonally) from the first small square. Pin the squares to keep them from shifting. The two small squares will overlap a bit in the middle. Placing a pin at the corners that overlap helps maintain the straight line while stitching. Draw a line with a mechanical pencil diagonally through the center of both of the small squares. This can be done with the Quick Quarter ruler. If you have had problems with accuracy when sewing against a single line drawn corner to corner, use the Quick Quarter to draw the sewing lines. Position the slots in the center of the ruler exactly at the corners of the square and draw a line on both sides of the Quick Quarter. Stitch a scant ¼″ seam on both sides of the line, or one thread inside the line if you drew both lines. Remember that a scant ¼″ is a needle width smaller than the line.

Small squares positioned on large square; line drawn and sewn

Cut the unit in half on the line (center) with your rotary cutter and ruler. Carefully press the seam allowance toward the two small triangles. Starch lightly and press dry. The units will have a heart shape once pressed.

Press toward small triangles.

Place another small square on the bottom of the large triangle, right sides together. One corner of the small square will extend past the point where the two small triangles are joined. Draw another line diagonally through the small square. Pin if needed. Stitch a scant ¼″ on both sides of the line.

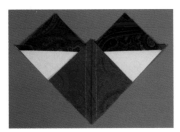

Drawn line and seam sewn

Cut the unit in half on the line that you drew. Press the seams toward the small triangles. If you have cut, sewn, and pressed very carefully and accurately, you will have four accurate Flying Geese units.

Finished goose

tip If the units do not finish to the exact measurement, check your seam allowance width. If you have been using tape or another type of barrier guide attached to the bed of your machine, you may find these types of processes can be a bit of a problem for accuracy. Because you are now sewing against a line instead of against the barrier, your seam allowance might not be accurate. If you consistently use a scant ¼″ seam allowance, you might not be taking enough seam allowance to accommodate the predetermined size needed for the process. Make a sample using a slightly larger as well as a slightly smaller seam allowance and see if the geese turn out more accurately. Once you find exactly where to place your foot against the line—and find which foot works the best for this process—you will be able to get the accuracy needed.

LESSON FOUR:

Flying Geese templates

Our personal favorite method for making Flying Geese was developed by Loretta Smith. Al Miller developed a trueing-up template to work with Loretta's technique that is super-accurate. When Al decided not to make the templates anymore, we decided to develop our own line of templates in order to keep them available. (For templates, see Resources, page 128.) Eleanor Burns with Quilt in a Day also has similar Flying Geese rulers. The main difference between the two types is the lines on ours are laser cut, so you can see exactly where to place the line on the seam. The Quilt in a Day placement lines are printed, making them thicker so they cover the seam.

This technique makes four geese at a time, working with squares. You will first cut and sew two different-sized squares together, cut them apart, and resew. It is a very interesting—and extremely accurate—method for creating Flying Geese.

Using the chart below, determine which size Flying Geese unit you need to make and cut the two different-sized squares listed.

Flying Geese cutting chart for squares

Flying Geese	Goose	Background
¾" × 1½"	3" square	4½" square
1" × 2"	3½" square	5" square
1¼" × 2½"	4" square	5½" square
1½" × 3"	4½" square	6" square
1¾" × 3½"	5" square	6½" square
2" × 4"	5½" square	7" square
2¼" × 4½"	6" square	7½" square
2½" × 5"	6½" square	8" square
3" × 6"	7½" square	9" square
4" × 8"	9½" square	11" square

1. Visually center the smaller square over the larger square, right sides together. Draw a diagonal line from corner to corner. When you align the ruler with the corners of the larger square, make sure that the corners of the smaller square also align exactly. Pin the two squares together to prevent slippage. Stitch a ¼" seam on each side of the line.

Align squares and draw line.

2. Press to set the stitching. Cut on the diagonal line and open. Stand the large triangle up on the ironing board and press the seam allowance toward the larger triangle (the fabric that was the larger square). Lightly starch and press dry.

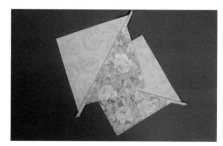

Press seam toward large triangle.

3. Place the two units right sides together so the opposite-colored fabrics are on top of each other, and match up the outside edges. The seams you stitched first will not butt or meet. There will be a gap between them. This is correct, even though it seems odd.

4. Draw a diagonal line perpendicular to (across) the first seams and then sew a ¼" seam on each side of the line.

Right sides together, line drawn

5. Cut on the diagonal line and press again, toward the fabric that was originally the larger square. You will get two geese from each half—a total of four for each set of squares.

Cut on line.

6. Fold each half in half and make a small clip at the fold in the seam allowance. Clip to the stitching.

Making clip

7. Press each half open, pushing the seam allowance toward the fabric of the larger square on each side. The clip allows the seam allowance to go both directions where needed.

Back of block to show pressing

8. Using the Flying Geese template, place the etched or printed lines over the seamlines. If you were very careful with the sewing and pressing of the squares, the seams should be right on the mark. The lines on the lower edge of the goose blocks need to be exactly aligned with the lines on the template. This establishes the perfect points on the bottom of the goose unit. The lines need to be exactly straight on the 45° seams up to the top point. The ruler adds the seam allowance beyond this top point.

9. Cut the right side first, then the top edge of the template. Turn the unit around and realign the template with the seams. Cut the bottom and the right side. You now have a perfect goose—actually four of them at a time.

Aligning template onto seamlines to cut

> **tip** A rotating mat or a small mat on top of your large mat is helpful when trimming the geese. You don't have to move the template to cut each of the four sides.

LESSON FIVE:

Foundation piecing Flying Geese

Sew and Fold on a Roll is the brand name of the first product on the market to paper piece Flying Geese. If you have tried foundation piecing, you might very well like making your geese this way. If you purchase the paper on a roll, making 18 geese at a time can become very cumbersome. We suggest 3–6 geese at a time so that you can manage the awkwardness of the paper. Once you get the hang of the process, longer strips of paper might become more manageable.

METHOD ONE: USING SEW AND FOLD ON A ROLL PREPRINTED PAPER

To make 18 geese, cut the paper so that you have 3 pieces, each containing 6 geese. Precut the fabrics into triangles to speed up the process. Cut the goose triangles from a square measuring 5¼″; cut diagonally twice corner to corner. The background triangles are cut from a square measuring 2⅞″ cut diagonally once, corner to corner.

Experiment with different needle sizes to see which makes holes that make tearing away the paper most easily after stitching. We personally prefer a size 70 needle with 60/2 machine embroidery thread and your machine set on a stitch length of 1.5.

You will be sewing on the printed side of the paper.

1. Place the first goose triangle face up along the horizontal line at the bottom of the paper. It should fit exactly to the printed large triangle (printed half dark blue and half light blue). Pin in place or use a dab of gluestick to keep it in place.

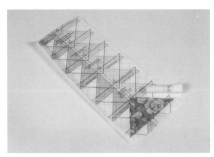
Placement of first goose triangle

2. Position the left background triangle, right side down, along the darker blue guide. Be sure to keep all the cut edges aligned perfectly. Pin to keep in place. Sew ¼″, keeping aligned with the dotted lines.

Positioning small triangle on paper

3. Open the small triangle and press. The edges of the small triangle should align exactly with the dark blue paper placement.

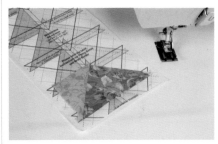
Small triangle opened

It is a good idea to try this as a test before starting a row of geese. The thread weight and the size of seam you take can negatively affect the result. If you sew exactly on the line, but the small triangle is too small when opened, the thread might be too heavy, or the seam too deep; sew a smaller seam allowance. If the small triangle is too large, you need to sew a deeper seam allowance. Practice until you find exactly where to stitch before making multiples.

4. Next, place a small triangle on the right side of the large goose triangle and align the edges with the light blue triangle on the paper. Pin to secure it. Stitch with your corrected seam allowance. Open and press. Once you get the correct seam allowance established, everything should fit exactly from here on.

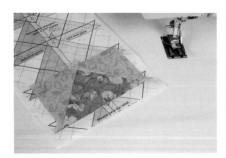

One complete goose

5. Next, position a large triangle, right side down, on top of the complete goose. Use the dark black lines for placement. Stitch the complete length of the triangle.

Position of second goose

6. Fold the triangle up and press firmly. Pin to hold it in place.

Large triangle pressed up

7. Now you are ready to continue with the rest of the geese in the row of paper. You will soon be flying through them as you get a rhythm for the back-and-forth movement of adding triangles.

8. Once the small units are finished, measure 2¼″ from the center point of each goose to each side and trim.

Trimming sides

9. Join the goose units end to end for a length of 18 geese. Carefully remove the paper from the back. If your stitches were small enough, the paper will remove easily. If you find it difficult to pull out, fold the paper back on itself and crease it.

METHOD TWO: MAKING YOUR OWN FOUNDATION PAPER

If you choose to make your own paper foundation, take a piece of ¼″ grid graph paper and draw a rectangle 4″ × 6″. Next, divide the rectangle into 3 equal 2″ sections.

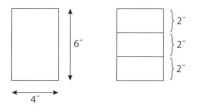

Draw a rectangle and divide it.

Divide the 2″ sections into triangles, as shown. Add a ¼″ seam allowance around the outside edge of the original rectangle.

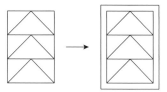

Draw in triangles and add seam allowance.

Quilt shops sell several different plain papers packaged expressly for creating your own paper piecing patterns. Other papers to try are doctors' examining room paper, quilt-and-tear paper, freezer paper, tissue paper, and washaway paper. Experiment to see if any of these will work well for you.

Experiment with different needle sizes as well as different paper types and weights for the combination that allows the paper to tear away most easily after stitching. We personally prefer a size 70 needle with 60/2 machine embroidery thread and the machine set on a stitch length of 1.5. For stiffer papers like freezer paper, you might need to go to a 75 needle and 60/3 sewing thread. Experiment until you find the combination that works best for you.

It is helpful to precut fabric for the areas instead of guessing what size and shape is necessary. We recommend that you cut the squares more than 1″ larger than the measurement for the small triangles—cutting a square and slicing it in half diagonally. For the geese, cut squares 1½″ larger than the width of the unit. (In this case the unit is 4″, so cut a square more than 5½″ and cut twice diagonally.) You need a total of 36 small light triangles and 18 large dark triangles. These pieces are larger than we had you cut for the Sew and Fold on a Roll paper, as you don't have all the guidelines marked, and you are working upside down. There is more margin for error doing this, and the larger sizes accommodate the potential for problems. You will be trimming the seam allowances in this method.

1. If you're making your own foundation paper, you'll be placing the fabric on the blank side of the paper and sewing on the lines on the opposite side. A tiny dot of gluestick can help hold triangle #1 in position. Holding the paper up to a light can be helpful to make sure the fabric is positioned correctly and that at least ¼″ of fabric extends beyond the stitching line on all sides.

Position large triangle on blank side of paper.

2. Position the fabric for triangle #2.

Position triangle #2.

3. Flip the paper foundation over to the printed side with the lines and stitch on the line between triangles #1 and #2. Fold the paper back along the stitched seam. Position a rotary ruler along the fold and trim the seam allowance to ¼″. Your Perkins Dry Goods Perfect Piecing Seam Guide is a great little ruler to trim seam allowances.

Trimming seam allowance

4. Open the little triangle so that it covers paper triangle #2 and finger press firmly. Position the fabric triangle #3 on the other side of triangle #1, matching the raw edges. Sew. Turn over and fold back the paper. Trim the seam allowance to ¼″, open triangle #3, and finger press. Continue in this manner until the foundation is covered.

5. Once you have added all the triangles to the paper foundation, press the entire unit while the paper is still in position. Trim around the outside edge of the foundation on the cutting line. Continue this process until you have 18 geese. Join the small units together to make one long row of geese. Press carefully. Remove the paper.

Designing with Flying Geese

Once you are hooked on making Flying Geese units, you will start to see them used for borders, sashing, and blocks with multiple small triangles within the goose triangle and for elements of many patchwork blocks. There are endless possibilities for how you can arrange the geese to give very different designs. Don't miss the joy of playing with all the potential you have with these fun pieces.

Below is a quilt that Harriet made using geese for sashing. Notice that the sashing between the blocks is a different size than the sashing between the rows. These geese are not standard size. They are drafted to the size needed for the size of the Nine-Patch block. The joy of being able to draft the geese is that they can be any size or dimension you need or want.

Homeward Flight

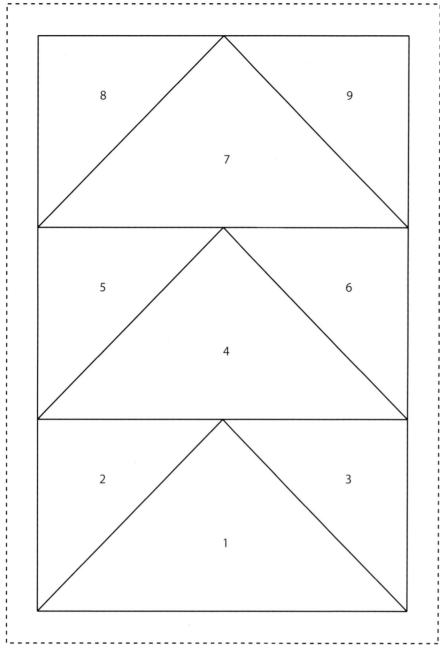

Sample of foundation needed for project

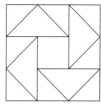

Ribbon

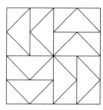

Dutchman's Puzzle

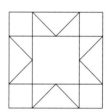

Sawtooth Star

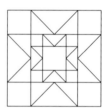

Rising Star

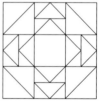

Cut the Corners

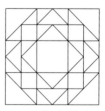

Aunt Sukey's Choice

There are an amazing number of traditional pieced blocks that have geese units in them. To the right are some of them for you to play with. We have scaled them to 1″ so that you can photocopy them and drop them into the worksheets you have in *Quilter's Academy,* Volume 2, Class 250 (pages 55–63). As you study the blocks below, you will start to see that different methods of making geese come into play for different designs. Even a combination of techniques might be called for in some block designs.

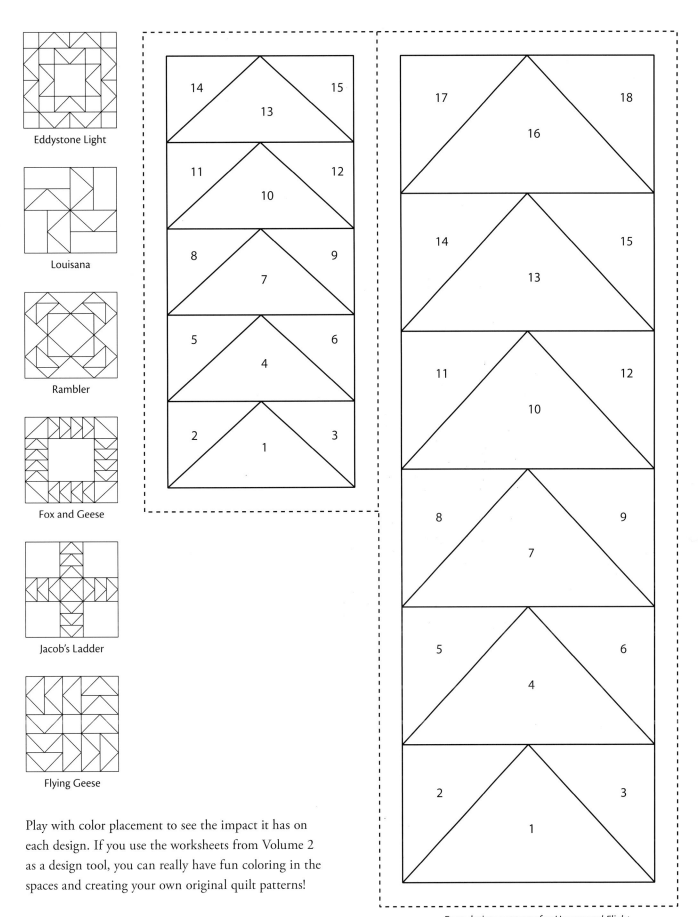

Eddystone Light

Louisana

Rambler

Fox and Geese

Jacob's Ladder

Flying Geese

Play with color placement to see the impact it has on each design. If you use the worksheets from Volume 2 as a design tool, you can really have fun coloring in the spaces and creating your own original quilt patterns!

Foundation patterns for *Homeward Flight*

LESSON SEVEN:
The quilts

CAT TRACKS AND BIRD TRAILS

You will use the geese units that you made from the 4 methods in this Class, Lessons Two to Five. Sew all the geese from each technique into a row of 18 geese. This makes the bars in the quilt. Carrie has done her quilt with "scrappy" geese. She did 24 scrappy single geese using the method in Lesson Two (page 70) so she could mix up the colors. For the methods in Lessons Three and Four, she made only 16 geese: 1 set of 4 geese from a square for each for the 4 colors. With this and the extra single geese from Lesson Two, you'll have enough geese for each row to have 18 geese and to mix up the colors. The foundation piecing row she again made using individual scrappy geese.

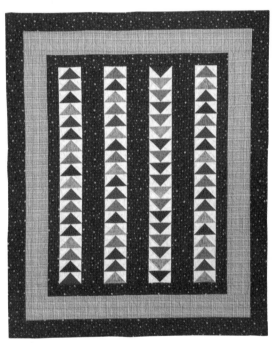

Cat Tracks and Bird Trails

Quilt top size: 46″ × 54″

Grid size: 2″ × 4″ Flying Geese

Geese units needed: 72

Yardages for quilt top:

⅓ yard each of 4 colors for scrappy geese
or ½ yard for single-color geese

⅔ yard cream background

1⅓ yards brown print for bars and borders

⅝ yard of tan plaid for second border

Constructing rows of geese

When sewing the individual geese together, be sure that the unit that shows the top point of the goose is on top. When stitching 2 units together, stitch a thread's width beyond the tip of the point of the goose (large triangle). This allows for a bit of easement when the seam is pressed. If the point is missing, take the stitching out and try again, this time stitching a bit farther away from the point. If there is too much space beyond the point, take a bit deeper seam allowance. Press the seam allowances up toward the large triangle.

When assembled, you should have 4 rows of 18 geese each. Each row should be 36½″ long.

> *note*   *We find that many students find the paper-pieced row to be either a bit shorter or longer than the individually constructed geese rows. If this happens to you, gently ease the extra in when the bars are sewn together. If you carefully distribute the fullness evenly the full length of the row, you will not notice that it was a bit different in the beginning.*

Adding solid bars

The bars in between the rows of geese are cut 4½″ wide. You will need to cut 3 strips 4½″ × 36″. You might want to consider cutting the strips a bit longer, making a mark at the additional length added to the top and bottom of the strip. When you pin the rows together to sew, align the marks with the top and bottom of the geese row. Pin the rows together carefully. Once sewn, this extra can be trimmed away to ensure that the strip is straight across the top and bottom of the quilt top before adding borders. Press all the seams to the solid bars. Starch lightly.

Adding borders

Once the bars are sewn together, it is time to add the borders. The first brown border is 2″ wide finished. Cut 2 strips 2¾″ × 37″. Mark ½″ on both ends of each strip. Place this mark at the top and bottom of the row of geese. Pin the strips in place and sew to the side of the goose row. Press to the border strip and starch lightly, pressing dry. Once both sides are added, square the bottom and top by trimming off the extra added for this purpose. Be sure to square off the seam. Trim the borders down to 2¼″ wide.

Measure across the width of the quilt top, raw edge to raw edge. Cut 2 strips 2¾" wide by the width of the quilt top, plus 1". Repeat the process above. Press toward the border, square the corners, and trim the width to 2¼".

The cream border is 4" finished. Repeat as above to add to the quilt top.

The final border is 3" finished. Remember to add at least 1"–2" extra to the width for ease in quilting. This will be cut away after the quilting is finished.

CARRIE'S WINTER GOOSE CHASE

Carrie's *Winter Goose Chase*

Quilt top size: 42½" × 53"

Grid size: 1½"

Blocks: 12

Yardages for quilt top:

¾ yard blue for geese and second border

1⅛ yards cream for background of geese

1½ yards shirting print for large squares and border

¾ yard brown print

Here's another fun skill-building Flying Geese quilt. You choose your favorite method for creating the 144 geese needed or the 48 three-goose units. The yardage above is figured if you are doing the method from Lesson Four (page 72). And you have a choice of ways to construct this quilt.

Carrie's quilt is constructed like a traditional Wild Goose Chase block, but you can also create this quilt by making the goose strips into sashing and having a solid square of shirting fabric between those sashes. Either way will get you the same end result, but if you choose to make Flying Geese sashes, you will need to write your own quilt recipe and alter the yardages given above.

These instructions are for constructing the quilt in blocks.

Again, to start, pick your favorite method for making Flying Geese. The finished size of the geese for this quilt is 1½" × 3", and you will need 144 of them total.

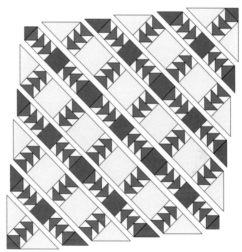

Alternate piecing layout

Once you have your geese constructed, you will need to sew them together in sets of 3 so that you have 48 of these sets, 4 for each of the 12 blocks.

You will now need to cut the 12 – 3½" squares that are in the center of each of the blocks and add 2 Flying Geese units to 2 opposite sides of the square. Press your seam allowance to the square and starch.

Goose/square/goose units

Now you will need to cut the large squares of the shirting print and then cut them into 4 triangles to get the setting triangles for the blocks. We figured these squares to be extra-large so that you can trim them down to size once the block is completed to ensure that your blocks are completely accurate for sewing together. You need 12 – 8½″ squares cut in half on both diagonals.

Add 2 triangles to each side to the remaining 24 three-goose units, pressing your seam allowances towards the triangles. Starch.

Triangle/goose/triangle units

Next, you will construct the main part of your Winter Goose Chase block, sewing 1 of the triangle/goose/triangle units to one side of the goose/square/goose units, making sure that you match and nest the seam allowances where the square from the long narrow unit meets the geese from your triangle/goose/triangle units. Press the seam allowance toward the large triangles and starch. Then add the second triangle/goose/triangle to the other side of the unit you just constructed.

Adding second triangle/goose/
triangle unit to block

Now you need to cut the brown triangles to make the block square. You need 24 – 5½″ squares that you will cut in half once diagonally to create the 48 triangles you need. Again, these squares are cut extra-large so what when you trim the blocks to size, they come out straight and accurate. Once these are cut, you will need to trim the excess fabric from the shirting triangles flush with the ends of the geese units.

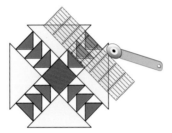

Trimming extra fabric away

Then fold the brown triangles in half along the long side and mark the center point. Line this up with the center of your goose units; pin and sew. Add the corners to all 12 blocks. Press the seam allowance toward the brown triangle and starch. Now it is time to trim. Your blocks should end up right around 11⅛″ square. When you trim, be sure to line up as many lines of your ruler with as many of the horizontal and vertical seams as you can.

It's time to construct your quilt top. The trickiest part of putting these blocks together is aligning the corners of the blocks, as you have 3 different points coming together for each block. Remember how we used a pin through the point to check alignment in Class 330, Lesson Six, page 50, for the *Spring Has Sprung* quilt? You will be doing the same thing here, but not only do you have to watch out for where the brown points meet but that the blue of the geese makes a nice straight line where the blocks meet. This will take a bit of patience but is worth it in the end.

Once the body of your quilt is done, it is time to add the first border. This border is special because it is pieced, using solid pieces and Flying Geese units so that the triangles on the edge of the quilt top will be completed into squares.

To figure what size Flying Geese you need to make, measure the height of one of the triangles along the edge of your quilt. Carrie's measured 2¼″. Subtracting the ¼″ seam allowance meant she needed to make 2″ × 4″ geese. A total of 14 of these are needed.

To make the corners, you also need to construct 4 half-square triangle units. Pick your favorite technique for making those—they need to finish at 2″ square.

To determine the length of the solid shirting piece to go between the Flying Geese border units, measure the long edge of one of the shirting triangles in the interior of the quilt. It should measure near 6½″; yours may be closer to 6⅜″. Whatever your measurement is, add ½″ for seam allowance and cut 14 of these rectangles.

Once you have your Flying Geese constructed, make each of the border strips, 2 for the top and bottom and 2 for the sides.

Add the side borders on first and then add the top and bottom. Then add the other borders as you have before, and you have completed another great quilt top! Congrats!

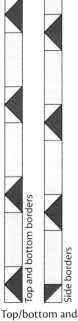

Top/bottom and
side border units

Class 360

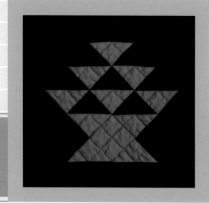

Figuring yardage for triangles

Figuring the yardage for triangles is a bit different from figuring for strips. Different techniques require different cut units, so before you can figure yardage, you need to determine which technique you are going to be using. We will go through each of the techniques and explain how you would come up with the yardage needed.

As a general guideline, you can work with a strip method to see how many squares will be cut from a strip the size of the triangle plus seam allowances. Because we use a 1″ measurement added to the finished size so that there is enough for trimming, determine the cut size of the squares needed and figure on getting 2 triangles from each square. If you have a block that uses 72 pink and 36 white 2″ finished triangles, how much fabric would it take? Let's walk through the formula using the pink fabric. A finished 2″ triangle would come from a 3″ square cut in half diagonally corner to corner. If you get 2 triangles from a square, and you need 72 triangles, use the following formula:

72 ÷ 2 = 36 squares. The squares are cut 3″, and each strip is about 42″ long.

42 ÷ 3″ = 14 squares from a strip. 36 ÷ 14 = 2.57 or 3 strips of fabric 3″ wide for the pink block.

If you are making a quilt with 13 of these blocks, we can rework the formula:

72 (1 block) × 13 = 936 triangles needed ÷ 2 (triangles per square) = 468 squares.

468 ÷ 14 (squares from a strip) = 33.43 or 34 strips × 3″ wide = 102″ ÷ 36″ (1 yard) = 2.83 or 2⅞ yards of pink. You would repeat this formula for the white to get the yardage needed for the white triangles.

If you decide on a technique to make your half-square triangles, you can figure the yardage based on the technique. For example, if you plan to use any of the techniques in Class 310, you would use the formula above for individual triangles cut from strips.

However, if you use the techniques from Class 320, you can approach this a bit differently.

Sheeting works with large pieces of fabric—up to 18″ × 22″. Using the same quilt idea as above, but this time we know we need 36 half-square triangle squares per block, and we have 13 blocks:

36 × 13 = 468. We know we get 2 units from each square drawn on the fabric, so divide 468 by 2, which equals 234. If we use fat quarters, we can get 6 squares drawn across the 18″ side and 7 squares along the 22″ side, giving us a total of 42 squares per fat quarter: 234 ÷ 42 = 5.57 or 6 fat quarters (1½ yards each) needed for the half-square triangle squares of pink and white. If individual triangles are added to the half-square units in the block, figure for them using strips.

We have provided you with a yardage chart for the Bias Strip method, to make this easy. Refer to the charts in Class 320, pages 23 and 24, to see what size squares are needed to yield the amount of triangles needed.

Eight triangles from a square is an easy one. If you get 8 half-square triangles from 1 square, refer to the chart in Class 320, page 25, to see what size square is needed to arrive at the size half squares desired. Let's use the same quilt again as before. We need 468 half-square triangle units. 468 ÷ 8 = 59 squares. If we need the units to finish at 2″, they need to be cut 6″ square. You can get 7 – 6″ squares from a 42″ strip of fabric.

59 ÷ 7 = 8.43 or 9 – 6″ strips = 54″ of fabric ÷ 36″ = 1½ yards of both pink and white.

Triangle paper would be figured by measuring how many triangles are printed on the paper within the length of a strip of fabric. Take the number of triangles you get from 1 strip and divide it into the total number of triangles needed. Multiply this number, which would be the number of strips needed, by the width of the strip needed.

Figuring yardage takes some time, but if you do not do it yourself, you can never be sure that the yardage stated on a pattern is sufficient for the technique you are choosing to use in construction of the quilt. Don't forget that you are also making a recipe as you go, so you will have a cutting chart as well as totals for each different unit once you are done. Not bad for a bit of calculator work.

LESSON TWO:
Borders with triangles

Pieced borders can add a lot of interest to the edges of your quilt tops, as you found out doing the simple pieced border on *Winter Goose Chase* in the last class (page 80). The potential for pieced border patterns seems endless. Any pieced block that you design or choose for your quilt contains elements that can be used for a pieced border. These borders can be as simple as squares sewn side by side or can be extremely complex.

We are introducing simple pieced borders that use half squares, quarter squares, three-piece triangle squares, and Flying Geese elements. We hope this whets your appetite for more designs and techniques as you go. Volume 5 is going to be all about medallion quilts and how to draft the endless borders that make them happen, so by the time you get set-in piecing under your belt in Volume 4, we hope you will be more than ready for the challenge of so many different pieced border options.

The Sawtooth design has many variations and is probably one of the most common borders that you see so often. The Sawtooth consists of half-square triangles lined up on their short sides, alternating light and dark. This border is very adaptable in size, style, and overall design. Following are several ideas for arranging the triangles for this border. Pay close attention to the corner treatment.

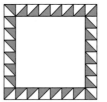

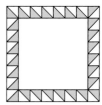

Triangles are going clockwise, corners are running with the direction of the triangles.

Counterclockwise, corners are still running with the triangles.

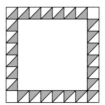

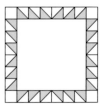

Corners opposite each other are the same— two different corners.

Changing direction in center gives four corners that are the same.

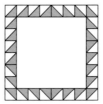

Same idea as above: triangles are turned the opposite direction.

Triangles placed in zigzag formation

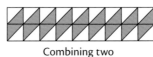

Combining two rows of triangles to get diamonds

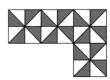

Two rows combined to get pinwheels

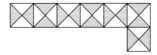

Alternating quarter-square units

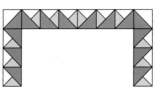

Three-piece triangle squares changing direction at center point

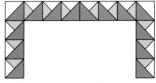

Three-piece triangle squares going the opposite direction as border on left

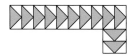

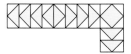
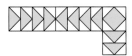

Flying Geese going
one direction

Flying Geese with square-in-
a-square corner treatment

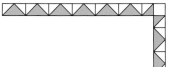

Flying Geese changing course
in center and use of square-
in-a-square units in corners

Flying Geese changing
course in center going
the opposite direction

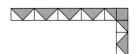

Flying Geese laid end to end,
using two half-square units
and a square in the corner

Using only one half
square unit in the corner

Using three half-square
units in the corner

Using two half square units
and one square in corner

Okay, now that you are probably excited to see how all the units you learned to make in the earlier classes can be put to use in borders, you are probably thinking of how to make them fit your quilt top! We personally prefer to work everything out on graph paper. There are several ways to approach this to keep it as simple as possible. We will save the math for Volume 5.

You can start by designing the border at the same time you plan the quilt top. If you work out the complete top on graph paper, a lot of the guesswork is taken out of your quiltmaking. Problem areas and filling spaces can be worked out and solved before you cut and piece anything. We can't stress enough how important precise piecing is to the planning and executing of pieced borders. You can imagine how difficult it would be to plan a quilt border to scale and then find that the blocks that determined that scale are not accurate. You would have a very hard time making it all fit. All of the diagrams above were drawn on graph paper. Work with the different grids that come in the packet we have available (see Resources, page 128) to get the scale of the blocks and border to work together.

You might want to design the border first, work out the corners, and then fill in the interior of the space with

the quilt top design. This is also done on graph paper. However, you might find that you don't know what will look best on the border until the quilt top is finished. It will still be easiest if you have planned the sizes of each unit and the layout on graph paper before you start.

Some quilters like to get the quilt top done, then measure the edges, and start the process from there. If this is how you plan to approach the process, be sure that the quilt top is very well pressed and starched so that the edges are flat and even, both sides are exactly the same length, and the top and bottom are the same width. You will need to do this whether you are working with graph paper or not.

Measure the length of the sides of the quilt top. Next, determine the size of each unit in the border—the repeat length. This is generally relative to the grid size used within the quilt top for the blocks. Divide the unit length into the border length needed. You are hoping that the unit divides evenly. The tricky part is to get both the top and bottom, as well as the side borders, to fit evenly. This is where working it out on graph paper can help you determine if you need a small strip border to work as a spacer to get the numbers to work happily for you. Don't worry about the corners at this point. They will be the size determined by the width of the border pieces.

If you cannot divide the number evenly, an easy way to handle the situation is to use a spacer (a different design unit) in the center of each of the sides. This will allow you to keep the original unit to size and fill in the gap with something else. Square in a Square blocks work really well for this. They don't have to be square but can take on the shape of diamonds of any angle to fill the space. Examine the borders of *Goose in the Pond,* in Class 390, page 124, which is your Final project. You will see these units in the center of each of the Flying Geese borders. They not only let the geese change direction, but take up the odd measurement that a goose would not fit in.

You will find that the spacing will not always come out exact, but there might be only $\frac{1}{16}$" or $\frac{1}{8}$" leftover. This tiny amount can be eased in as you sew the borders onto the quilt top. Anything up to $\frac{1}{4}$" can be done this way; anything larger will need to be drafted to add a spacer or change the size of the unit. Easing in too much will cause the outside edge of the border to have a wave that will always be a problem.

LESSON THREE:
Internal frames with triangles

Here you will find a variety of internal frames constructed using triangles. With the addition of triangles, the possibilities of these frames become endless. This is another great place to play with the design sheets and graph paper to create your own unique designs.

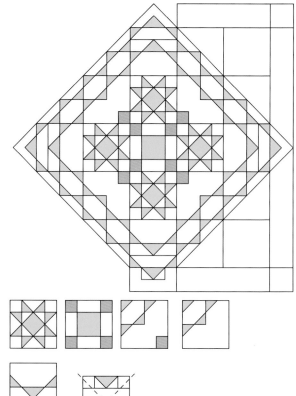

Block/border combo 2

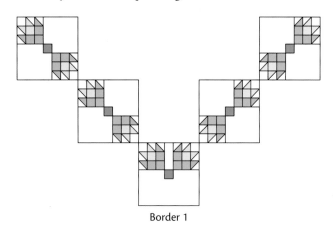

Border 1

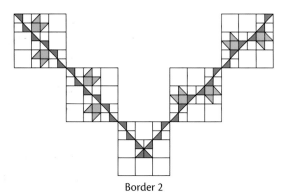

Border 2

Block/border combo 3

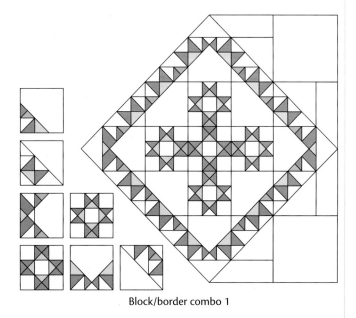

Block/border combo 1

LESSON FOUR:
The quilts

In this lesson you will make two quilts that have internal frames made using triangles.

CARRIE'S BEACHY SNAIL'S TRAIL

Carrie's *Beachy Snail's Trail*

Quilt top size: 60″ × 70½″

Grid size: 2″

Blocks:

18 block 1

17 block 2

Yardages for quilt top:

1¼ yards teal polka dot

¼ yard light teal swirl

⅔ yard dark teal (includes yardage needed for border)

¼ yard cream

2 yards tan

This first quilt is basically a Square in a Square block. Like *Winter Goose Chase,* this quilt can be constructed two different ways: either as very large Square in a Square blocks

or as Square in a Square blocks with linking blocks of quarter-square triangles. The latter is the method Carrie chose, as it makes constructing the border a little easier and more straightforward. Look at the previous photo and see if you can pick out the two ways you could make this quilt. Try drawing it out on your graph paper and see which method makes the most sense to you.

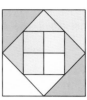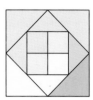

Color variations A, B, and C for *Snail's Trail* block 1

Color variations D, E, and F for *Snail's Trail* block 2

To start making your blocks, construct the 2 different color combinations of four-patches that you need to make Block 1, tan and teal polka dot and cream and teal polka dot.

It's been awhile since we have made four-patches. For a refresher go back to Volume 1, Class 150, Lesson Six (pages 56–58).

Once your four-patches are made, it is time start making them a square into a square. Following the instructions on page 38 in Class 330, Lesson Three, add the first round of triangles to your four-patch units. Be mindful of the 3 different colorways of blocks you have. You may want to separate these into 3 different stacks to keep straight which color triangle you are adding to which side. Refer to the previous illustration of block 1 for guidance. You will need to cut 13 squares of cream and 5 squares of tan 4″ square and then cut these in half once diagonally. Refer again to the illustration of colorways for block 1, making sure that you sew the cream triangles on the appropriate side of the four-patches.

All 18 four-patches will get a cream triangle on one side; 8 will then get a second cream triangle on the opposite side, and 10 will get a tan triangle. Make sure you fold the triangles in half on the long edge and mark the halfway point so you can line this up with the seamline of the four-patches.

Once you have these triangles sewn to 2 sides of the four-patches, press the seam allowance toward the triangles and starch. Trim the points that extend beyond the four-patches and other remaining 2 sides. You will now need to cut 16 – 4″ squares of the light teal swirl and 2 – 4″ squares of tan. All 18 of the blocks will get a light teal triangle on one side. The opposite side of 14 blocks will also be light teal. The remaining 4 blocks get a tan triangle. Again, be careful with the color placement. Refer to the illustrations to make sure the triangles are going on the correct sides. Press and starch, and now you are ready to trim this first round down to size.

Line the ¼″ line of your favorite square ruler up with the points of four-patches and trim the top and right side of your block that extends past the ruler.

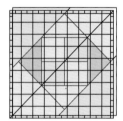

Ruler alignment with four-patch points

Turn your blocks 180°, realign the ruler, and trim the remaining two sides.

Now you are ready to cut and sew the last round of triangles on to complete block 1. All the squares for this round will be cut 5¼″ and then cut in half once diagonally. Again, all 18 blocks will have a cream triangle on one side, 14 will have a cream triangle on the opposite side, and the remaining 4 will have tan on the opposite side.

The same as you did on the last round, watch the color placement.

Mark the middles of each triangle and align the mark with the points of four-patches; pin in place and sew.

Press toward the triangle, starch, and trim the extra fabric extending past the next sewing edges. The last round is the same as the last 3: all blocks have one side with a dark teal triangle, 8 blocks will have a second dark teal triangle, and the remaining 10 blocks will have a tan triangle as the last triangle you add to the blocks.

Press, starch, and then trim. Your blocks should be 8½″ square once you have trimmed them, again aligning the ¼″ line of the ruler with the point of the previous round.

Now it's time to make the linking blocks. Remember the quick and easy method you learned in Class 340, Lesson Two, page 55? Make these units a little larger than needed so you can trim them to be the exact size to match your finished blocks. Carrie started with 10″ squares. Refer to the illustration for block 2 for the 3 different colorways needed.

You get 2 quarter-square triangle units for each set of squares you sew. Cut 6 teal polka dot / cream square combinations, 2 teal polka dot / tan combinations, and 1 cream/tan combination. Layer the 2 squares for each combination together and mark a diagonal X on 1 of the fabrics. Pin the squares together and sew ¼″ on either side of one of the lines.

Once all the squares are sewn, cut them apart on both lines and press toward the darker of 2 triangles. Lay out the combinations according to the illustration for block 2 and construct these blocks, making sure that you nest the seam allowances and pin the

blocks to help keep the bias under control. With all the block 2's made, and making sure the seamlines are in the exact middle of the corners, trim your quarter-square triangle linking blocks to match the size if you pieced blocks and then construct the middle of your quilt top.

Now it is on to the border.

Again, because Carrie chose to construct this quilt using 2 different blocks rather than making large Square in a Square blocks, setting them on point, and making complicated internal frame blocks, we are going to create the same look of the complicated internal frame blocks but without the problems that can come from making those multi-unit difficult blocks.

You will first add a 2″ finished size border all the way around the quilt top. Now you will need to construct the braided ribbon border. Following are the illustrations of the 2 border units you will need to piece.

Side border units

Top and bottom border units with cornerstones

To make these borders, you need to construct the following units:

24 A/B units

24 C/D units

4 E/F units

2 G/J units

2 H/J units

2 H's

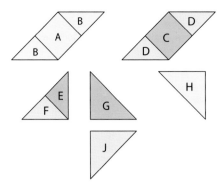

To make these units, you will need to cut 24 – 2½″ squares of both the teal polka dot and the dark teal.

You will also need 12 – 4″ squares of tan to be cut in half twice diagonally and 15 – 4″ squares of teal polka dot. Twelve of those 15 squares you will cut into quarters diagonally, and the other 3 you will only cut in half once diagonally.

Finally you need 2 – 4″ squares of dark teal (one will be cut in both directions diagonally, and the other will be cut once on the diagonal) and 2 – 4″ squares of tan, also only cut in half once diagonally.

Using the previous illustrations, construct your braided border and press all your seams toward the squares in each unit. Then assemble the units according to the border illustrations. Two of the E/F units, the 2 G/J units, the 2 H/J units, and the 2 H's make up the cornerstones that will be at the ends of the top and bottom borders. Make sure when you are done assembling the border strips that you turn them in the correct direction to make the braided pattern—2 of your corners should be green, and the other 2 should end in teal.

Once this is done, you are ready to pin and sew your borders to your quilt. Be sure to pin these borders onto your quilt top securely—they are heavy, and the fabric can tend to shift in transport between your cutting table and the sewing machine. Our suggestion is to have a pin in each triangle that touches the previous solid border.

The final solid border for this quilt was cut 6″ wide but trimmed to 4¼″ after the quilt was quilted.

We hope you have enjoyed making this mock internal frame and the *Snail's Trail* quilt top. If you want a challenge, make another small version of this quilt, but make it using the single block on point we talked about at the beginning of these instructions and figure out how to make the internal frame blocks and corners. See which method you like better.

CARRIE'S AMISH BASKETS

Carrie's *Amish Baskets*

Quilt top size: 34″ × 42½″

Grid size: 1½″

Blocks:

    12 design blocks

    6 alternate blocks

    10 internal frame blocks

    14 pieced setting triangles

    4 frame corners

Yardages for quilt top:

    ⅛ yard or fat quarters of at least 13 different bright solid colors*

    2 yards black solid

The thirteenth color is for the internal frame if you want to use a different color from the baskets.

This cheery little quilt is fun to make and gives you the good challenge of doing an internal frame using triangles. This is one of the easiest internal frame blocks you can do with half-square triangle units. The addition of the pieced setting triangles makes this border look more complicated than it really is.

However, before we delve into making the frame blocks, let's start with the basket blocks.

Please choose your favorite method of making half-square triangle units from Classes 310 and 320. The yardage for this quilt was figured based on the Eight from a Square method (page 25). If this method does not work for you, refigure the yardage for this quilt using your chosen method to be sure you will have enough fabric.

To start making this quilt, you will need to make 2 sets of the Eight from a Square method, so you will end up with 12–14 half-square triangle units of each of 12 different colors combined with the black. The grid size of

this quilt is 1½", so you should end up with 2" units. Be sure to consider this if you're working with a different method from what Carrie chose to use. To do the Eight from a Square method, you need to cut 24 – 6" squares of black and 2 – 6" squares of each of 12 colors. Pair up a colored square with a black square and mark an X on each set with a pencil. At the sewing machine, sew ¼" on both sides of both lines.

Once this is done, cut your squares apart to create the half-square triangle units. Cut the squares in quarters on the straight grain, top to bottom and side to side, as well as on both of your diagonal pencil lines. (Refer to page 25 for help if needed.)

Press your triangle seam allowances toward the black, starch, and trim your triangle units down to 2" square, making sure that the seam allowance is exactly in the corners.

You will also need to cut 1 – 2" square of each of the colors, as well as 1 – 2" square of the black and 48 rectangles 2¼" × 4". These are cut a little large so you can trim them down to be completely accurate after your blocks are done. You want to do this for this quilt because these 2 pieces are large solid units being sewn onto small units with lots of seams that can distort the large piece.

Now lay out your cut units according to the following illustration. You can easily just stack the units for all 12 blocks on top of one another and chain sew all 12 blocks at one time. You will have 2–4 extra colored half-square triangle units. Set these aside. You will use them when you make the tulip squares for the setting triangles.

Basket block layout

Once your pieces are all laid out, it's time to sew. The following is a series of illustrations that will guide you through the construction of your Basket blocks. The arrows in these illustrations indicate the direction you need to press your seam allowance.

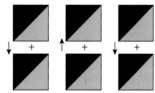

Basket block construction step 1

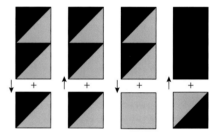

Basket block construction step 2

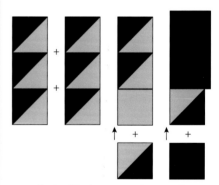

Basket block construction step 3

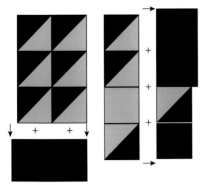

Basket block construction step 4

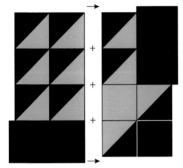

Basket block construction step 5

Once you have your blocks made, you need to trim down those extra-large rectangles.

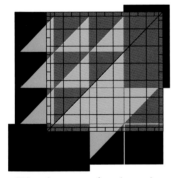

Trimming rectangle units to size

Now you can cut your solid alternate squares. Your blocks should measure 6½". If your blocks measure a little differently and are different consistently, cut your alternate squares to that size. If you only have 1 or 2 blocks that measure differently, check all your seams and make sure they are straight and don't bow in or flare out at the end. Fix any problem seams and remeasure.

Next, you need to construct the internal frame blocks. If you are using the Eight from a Square method, you will need to cut 5 – 6" squares of both the black and the last color from your selection so you have a total of 40 half-square triangle units.

These half-square triangle units get sewn into a four-patch unit with a solid black square, cut 2", and these 20 blocks will be sewn together with larger solid black squares cut 3½" to make the frame blocks.

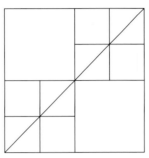

Internal frame block

Constructing the 4 frame corner blocks is next. You will need to make 16 more half-square triangle units. You will also need to cut 4 – 3½" × 2" rectangles and 8 – 2" squares of black to make half of the block. The other half of the block is a solid piece of black cut 3½" × 6½".

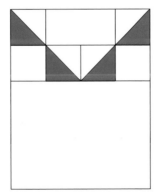

Internal frame corner block

The last blocks you need to make are the setting triangles. For these you will make the tulip square and then

add 2 smaller setting triangles onto these squares.

The tulip square is made from 2 of the colored half-square triangle units you made earlier and set aside, a colored square, and a black square. Construct these units.

Tulip square unit

Now you need to cut the setting triangles. Remember how to do this? It's been awhile since we did a diagonal set. For a refresher, refer to Volume 2, Class 230, Lesson Two (pages 23–26). The tulip square measures 3½". Take this measurement times 1.414, and you get 4.95 or 5"; add 1"–3", depending on how much you want your blocks to float in the black background. Carrie chose to only add an inch. Cut 7 squares the size you choose and cut them in half diagonally twice. Sew these to the 2 sides of the tulip block that are all black.

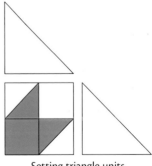

Setting triangle units

With all the different blocks made, you are ready to lay out your blocks and sew your quilt top together.

We hope you enjoyed making this fun little quilt!

Class 370

Mock Feathered Stars

Before we go into true Feathered Stars in Class 380, we are introducing you to another type of star that is equally striking—what we call mock Feathered Stars. These stars are completely made of half-square triangles, whereas Feathered Stars have a 45° diamond at the tip of each point. Mock Feathered Stars are generally drafted on an even grid, whereas Feathered Stars require an unequal grid and are much harder to draft. Mock Feathered Stars can have different sized half-square units in the same block just as Feathered Stars do, so be careful in trimming the half squares and keep them separated and marked to eliminate confusion.

We thought this would be a great place to have you jump into more complicated blocks without bogging you down with big quilts. These stars also prepare you for the more technical piecing needed for Feathered Stars. If you have worked through the quilts in this book up to this point, you are ready to apply that knowledge to this Class. By this time, we feel that if you want to turn any of these blocks into awesome quilts, you have the ability to do so if you have

worked through all three books. We have faith in you!

The projects you will be making to learn the techniques in this Class are not made into actual quilts. They could be small table toppers or wallhangings, but you might want to consider laying the blocks aside after you have completed them and use them as centers for the medallion quilts you will be designing in Volume 5.

tip We find that the most helpful tool to work with when making either mock Feathered Stars or Feathered Stars is Marsha McCloskey's Feathered Star Ruler, which is an 8½" ruler that measures in 1", ½", ¼", ⅛", and ¹⁄₁₆" increments. If you want true accuracy, this ruler makes it easy to cut the unfriendly ruler numbers you often come up with when drafting Feathered Stars.

INTRODUCTION TO STARS USING ONLY TRIANGLES

All of these blocks use many of the same-sized triangle units, so we have left it up to you to choose the techniques you would prefer to

construct these units. We are not going into detail on the construction of each block. We have broken out the units and have listed the cutting requirements for one block. General instructions are given on the breakout of the blocks; you can fill in the blanks for how to get to that point.

tip We suggest that you read all of the instructions before you start to cut and sew. We routinely cut the large side triangles and corner squares larger than is mathematically correct. We will give you the right measurements but suggest that you add 1" to what is listed for trimming. These triangles and corners tend to sew in small, and if they are not large enough to accommodate the points of the single triangles at the ends of the feather rows, the block will not be square, and you will lose your points on the outside edge of the block. There is also the problem of the long side of the triangle not staying straight and therefore needing to be trimmed. It is always easier to add too much and trim than to have the block not go together easily.

Consider this your midterm exam.

LESSON ONE:
Star Diamond

Star Diamond is a classic quilt block that was published in the April 1933 issue of *Ladies' Home Journal.* The original illustration of the quilt in that magazine was set on point with plain alternating blocks. It can also be set together as a straight set with sashing separating the blocks. We recommend that you make a sample block first and then create your own ideas with the worksheets in Volume 2, Class 250.

Star Diamond block

Star Diamond block

We have drafted this block to finish at 16⅞″ square. Study the block on graph paper and see if you can see how the lines connect and how you get the shapes and sizes. Everything is evenly divided, working off the corners of the basic nine-patch grid. Can you see how you get two different sizes of half-square triangles?

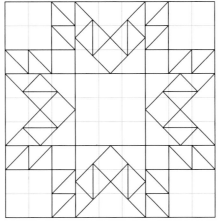

Drafted Star Diamond block

You will be working with 2″ and 1⅞″ finished units. Keep the units in 2 separate envelopes and mark each with its size. The larger half squares are used in Unit 1, and the smaller ones are used in Unit 2. We recommend that you work with either the Bias Square ruler or Marsha McCloskey's Feathered Star Ruler for this class, as they are marked for precision cutting of ⅛″ increments.

You will be able to make one star from a fat quarter of each fabric. We used a dark pink print, a brown print, a beige background and a fussy-cut panel for the center.

For one star—

Cut from dark pink:

4 – 3¾″ squares. Cut each square once diagonally into 8 triangles (G).

Cut from brown:

4 – 2⅞″ squares; cut once diagonally into 8 triangles (Unit 2—D).

Cut from background:

4 – 2½″ squares (Unit 2—E)

4 – 2⅜″ squares (Unit 1—B)

1 – 6⅞″ square; cut twice diagonally into 4 triangles (Unit 2—F). (Consider cutting larger—see tip above.)

4 – 4¼″ squares (Unit 1—C) (Consider cutting larger.)

From large print:

1 – 6⅛″ square (H)

Construct (using any technique you prefer):

8 – 2½″ half-square triangle squares (Unit 2—D)

16 – 2⅜″ half-square triangle squares (Unit 1—A)

Unit 1

Construct 4 of Unit 1 for each star you make. Unit 1 uses pieces A, B, and C.

Read all the instructions before you start anything.

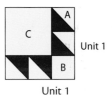

Unit 1

UNIT 1

Following the above diagram, lay out the 4 half-square triangle units, 1 B square, and 1 C square. Sew the half squares together in both rows. Add 1 set of half-square units to the side of C. Press the seam allowance toward the square (C). Add the B square onto the end of the remaining set of half-square triangles. Press toward the B square.

Add this unit to the lower edge of the C square, butting the seams carefully. Press toward the C square. Make four of these units.

tip We find that if you press the seam allowances of the feather units open as you construct the rows of feathers (half-square triangle units), it is easier to see the intersecting seams and hit them exactly when sewing the row of feathers onto the larger triangles. Press the seam allowance toward the single triangles. All the other seams are pressed the direction they tend to lie, or toward the large triangles.

note Check each side of each unit to ensure that the points of the triangles are exactly ¼″ from the raw edge.

UNIT 2

For Unit 2 you will need the remaining pieces except the center print (H). Lay out the pieces for one unit following the diagram below.

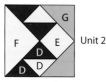

Unit 2

Join 1 half-square triangle unit to 1 single triangle for each side. Attach 1 of these units to the side of triangle F. Press toward the large triangle (F). Add the E square to the end of the remaining joined triangle unit. Press toward the square. Sew this unit to the other side of the F triangle. Add the G triangles, one at a time, to the opposite side of the half-square triangle units. Fold each G triangle

in half along the long side to find the center point and align it with the seam on the side of Unit 2.

Trim Unit 2 so that all the points are ¼″ from the raw edge, and the unit is 6⅛″ square.

ASSEMBLE THE STAR DIAMOND BLOCK

Using the diagram of the block above, lay out the 4 Unit 1 pieces in the corners and 4 Unit 2 pieces in between them, in 3 horizontal rows of 3 units each. Place the center square in the center of the block.

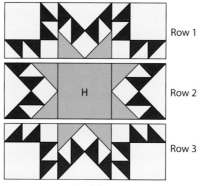

Block layout

Sew together the units in each row. Press the seam allowances in one direction, alternating with each row. Join the rows to make a Star Diamond block. As always, pay special attention to the points as you are joining units.

Now that you have made one block, are you up to making four or even twelve for a throw or a quilt? See the following two diagrams to inspire you.

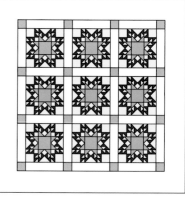

Star Diamond nine-block set with sashing

As you look at the illustration above, how would you change it or improve on it to suit your tastes? Play with some of these ideas:

❋ Use narrower sashing.

❋ Use no cornerstones.

❋ Windowpane the blocks.

❋ Make it very scrappy with different backgrounds and different triangle colors.

❋ Use a bold stripe border print in the center of the blocks and the border.

Star Diamond on point with alternating block

Again, as you look at the illustration, could you do anything to the design to jazz it up a bit? Work with Volume 2 and the worksheets to get some ideas going. Here are some options:

- ❊ Sashing
- ❊ Different fabric for setting triangles
- ❊ Internal frame added instead of plain borders
- ❊ Windowpaning
- ❊ Scrappy fabrics
- ❊ Solid alternate squares for a lot of heavy quilting

LESSON TWO:
Carrie's Star

We are adding a bit more detail to this star. Carrie drew this on graph paper years ago, and we thought it was a nice addition here. It is similar to Star Diamond; it just has more half-square triangle units in the points. We have gradated the colors from medium to light in the triangles to soften the lines a bit.

Quilt top size: 27″ × 27″

Grid size: 3″

Carrie's Star

Carrie's Star

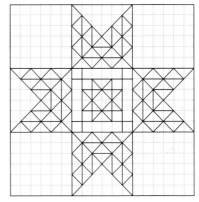

Drafted Carrie's Star

This block is again drafted on a nine-patch grid. We have assigned a size of 1½″ finished for the grid, as we know from the formula for Sawtooth Star that 1½″ gave us a ruler-friendly number for the half-square triangles.

The center of the star has a 9″ square. You can put anything in this space. You might want to interview different 9″ blocks, a panel print that can be fussy cut, another square in a square, an appliqué, or most anything else you like the looks of. We chose a simple 6″ star and surrounded it with a frame. Time to play with graph paper again!

Begin by choosing and constructing whatever you want in the center. If you are making the star we chose, you will be making a small square in a square, four Flying Geese units, and four squares.

❊ Construct a 3″ finished (3½″ cut) square-in-a-square unit for the center (Class 330, Lesson Three, page 38).

❊ Construct 4 Flying Geese units 1½″ × 3″ (Class 350, any method you choose).

❊ Cut 4 – 2″ squares for corners.

❊ Cut 4 – 2″ × 6½″ strips for star borders.

Lay the units out to form the block and sew them together into rows; then sew the rows together. The frame is cut 2″ for each of the 4 sides, with 4 – 2″ cut squares in the corners. The block should measure 9½″ exactly.

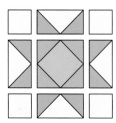

Center square

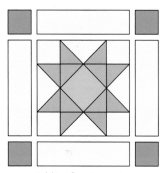

Adding framing strips

CONSTRUCTING THE STAR

Begin by counting how many half-square triangle units are needed in each color combination and how many single triangles are needed in each color. Here are the totals we came up with:

24 peach and white half-square triangles

12 yellow and white half-square triangles

12 white single triangles

24 green single triangles

Using your method of choice, construct the half-square triangles, making sure they are cut exactly 2⅝″, to finish at 2⅛″.

Cut:

12 green 3″ squares, cut in half diagonally for single triangles

6 white 3″ squares, cut in half diagonally for single triangles

For the outside corner squares and side triangles, cut:

4 – 9½″ squares of background (Consider cutting larger for trimming.)

1 – 10½″ square, cut in half diagonally twice (Consider cutting larger for trimming.)

1. Break the point units apart into 4 separate triangles: 1 background triangle and 3 pieced triangles. Using the diagram below, piece the triangles into rows and then connect the rows. There are 2 different layouts for this unit. Make 8 of the unit with the green single triangles and 4 of the unit with the white single triangles.

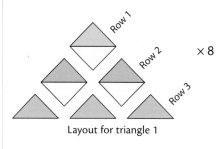

Layout for triangle 1

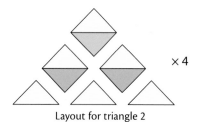

Layout for triangle 2

2. Once the triangles are pieced together, join the 4 units for each side unit.

3. Now you are ready to lay out all of the 9 units using the diagram below. Sew the units into rows and sew the rows together.

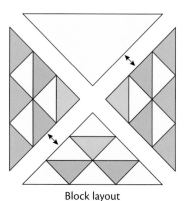

Block layout

Are they getting easier? Practice makes perfect. One more star to go, and you will be ready to tackle the real Feathered Stars in Class 380!

LESSON THREE:
Sawtooth Star

Sawtooth Star is a fairly simple-looking block, but there are some construction techniques that will be different from what you have done up to now. The pieces are larger than in the two previous stars, so you can have a short break from the small triangles; however, there are quite a few formulas to work through to see where we get the sizes to cut for each position in the star.

Sawtooth Star

16 ÷ 1.414 = 11.32 + .5 (seam allowance) = 11.82, or 11⅞″ cut for center square

11.875 (11⅞) ÷ 1.414 = 8.4 + .875 (seam allowance) = 9.27, or 9¼″ cut for corners on center square

Cut:

1 – 11⅞″ square fussy-cut fabric

2 – 9¼″ squares, each cut in half diagonally once

Using the instruction in Class 330, Lesson Two (page 37), construct the center square in a square. Trim the excess fabric of the corner triangles away to ¼″ from the points. Make sure the piece is a perfect 16½″ square. A 16½″ square ruler is a real asset for trimming squares this large.

From here on in, the rest of the cutting sizes will be figured using the center square measurements.

To find the size of the large triangles along the sides, take 16.875 (finished size of center square) plus seam allowance for a half-square triangle (.875); this equals 17.75.

Cut 1 – 17¾″ square background fabric; cut into quarters. (This number is larger than the mathematically correct 16⅞″, for trimming.)

Using the above findings, you can figure the size of the half-square triangle units. How do we figure out what size to make them?

11.93 (the short leg of the side triangle) – .875 (subtract the seam allowance) = 11.06 ÷ 4 (4 triangles on the side of the large triangle) = 2.75 (finished measurement of the

You will notice when you study the drafted version of this star that the center section is larger than the corner sections. Star Diamond and Carrie's Star are simple nine-patch squares, with three even divisions in each row. Sawtooth Star has five grids in the corners and eight grids in the center and side units. This is the basic format of a true Feathered Star, but the added diamond on each of the eight points of a Feathered Star makes the drafting much more difficult. Star Diamond ends up with two different-sized half-square triangles, whereas Sawtooth Star uses all the same size.

Sawtooth Star

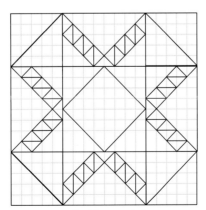

Drafted Sawtooth Star

We are going to walk you through how we came up with the sizes of the units as we go. The formulas will be messy, as we want you to understand what the numbers represent and where they came from. We will start with the center square in a square. By counting the squares on the graph paper, we find that feathers—or half-square triangles) + .5 (seam allowance) = 3¼″ cut half-square triangle units. Using any method of your choice, make:

24 – 3¼″ half-square triangles (cut measurements). These will finish to 2¾″.

For the single triangles at the end of each row and the triangle at the center:

2.75 (size of finished half squares) + .875 (⅞″ seam allowance for triangles) = 3⅝″ cut squares, cut in half diagonally.

Cut:

4 – 3⅝″ squares of blue; cut each square in half diagonally.

2 – 3⅝″ squares of background; cut each square in half diagonally.

The last pieces to cut for the side units are the smaller red triangles. What size are they?

2.75 (finished size of half-square triangle) × 3 (number along the diagonal side of the triangle) = 8.25 (finished measurement of the diagonal) ÷ 1.414 = 5.83 + .5 (seam allowance) = 6⅜″, or 6⅝″ if you want extra to trim and square up.

Cut:

4 – 6⅜″ squares of red; cut in half diagonally.

Now you are ready to assemble all these pieces into the side units. Follow the instructions carefully, as this is a bit different from the other piecing you have done up to now.

1. Join 3 half-square triangle units together as illustrated—one set the mirror image of the other. Repeat for the remaining three sides.

Join half-square triangles into threes.

2. Add the single blue triangles onto the ends. Be sure to carefully study the diagram so that you don't add them to the wrong end.

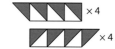

Add single blue triangle to one end of each unit.

3. Add a single white triangle to the opposite end of four of the above units. Make sure you are adding it to the same oriented pieces. Press toward the white triangle.

Adding white triangle

4. You are ready to add these units to the large triangle. They will be added to the short sides, which are bias. Handle with care. Take one of the strips without the white triangle and position it on the right side of the large triangle. See the illustration. Sew very carefully. Align the points exactly and pin in place to prevent slipping. Start sewing by turning the flywheel of the machine the first couple of stitches. These points are easily eaten by the machine. Press the seam allowance toward the large triangle.

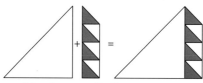

Adding first row of half-square triangles

5. Add the remaining strip of half squares to the other straight side of the large triangle. Align the points exactly and butt the seam of the small white triangle with the half-square triangle. Press toward the large triangle.

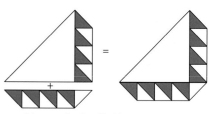

Add second side of half-square triangles.

6. The last thing to add to this unit is the smaller red triangles. One goes on each side of the half-square units. You can go back to the graph paper drafting of the star to determine the size this triangle needs to be. The short legs of the triangle are 3 grids. Each grid equals 2″, so the short legs are 6″ finished. For the triangle, add ⅞″ for seam allowances, both on the sides and the diagonal cut. If you want a bit extra for squaring and trimming, add 1″, or cut 7″.

Cut:

2 – 7″ squares of red, cut in half diagonally.

Adding red triangles to finish sides

Find the center of the row of feathers and the center of the long side of the red triangle. Mark and align the 2 pieces. Pin and sew the seam.

Once these triangles are sewn onto the edge of the feathers, check that the finished piece is 16½″ along both long edges and 10½″ on the short sides. Measure from the center out 8¼″ and square the edges to be exactly square and straight. If anything is a bit off, try using starch and gently persuade the piece to the correct size with heat and starch. Always use a very light misting of starch—do not make the fabric damp. This is what causes distortion when ironing. Because the measurements in the formulas are not exact ruler measurements, there are times when things don't fit exactly to the thread. Gentle persuasion is the order of the day.

Once these corners are attached, stitch 2 of these units to the sides of the center square-in-a-square unit.

CORNERS

Again, the drafted pattern will tell you that the corners use 5 grids × 2″, or 10″ squares finished. You will need 10⅞″ (or 11½″ for trimming) squares.

Cut 2 – 10⅞″ squares each of red and background fabric.

Pair 2 opposite color squares together, draw a line diagonally corner to corner, and sew ¼″ from both sides of the line. Cut on the line, press toward the red triangle, and trim to be exactly 10½″ square.

Now it is time to lay out the units to form the block.

Block layout

There are fewer seams to match here than on Star Diamond, but the ones to watch out for are:

* The points at the edges of the block
* The seams between the units (Check that they butt accurately.)
* The point of the square in a square

When joining the half-square corners to the center units, be sure you butt the diagonal seams at the outside edge in order to get a perfect ¼″ distance from the point to the outside cut edge.

Whew … was that fun! Ready for more?

LESSON FOUR:
Colonial Star

This last star combines many of the processes that made the previous stars go together. We are going to give you the measurements we used (2″ finished) and the breakouts, but no instructions. You can choose any grid you want to make any size quilt you want. There are no diagonal measurements in this pattern. All the half-square triangles are straight with the grid. You should be able to do the figuring and sewing sequences by now. Have fun!

Quilt top size: 40″ × 40″

Grid size: 2″

Colonial Star

Colonial Star

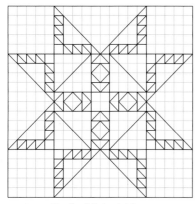

Drafted Colonial Star

Start by breaking the star apart into units. They are separated below. Count how many you need of each unit and determine what size you will need to cut your fabric to obtain the correct finished size. The units are on an even grid in the drafted illustration above. We assigned a 2″ finished size to each grid. The drafting is on 8-to-the-inch paper, so every two grids = 2″.

Center square

How many are there? _____

What is their finished size? _____

What is their cut size? _____

Square in a square from center of quilt

How many are there? _____

What is their finished size? _____

What is their cut size? _____

Flying geese units

How many are there? _____

What is their finished size? _____

What is their cut size? _____

Half-square triangle corners

How many are there? _____

What is their finished size? _____

What is their cut size? _____

Feather units

How many are there? _____

How many green and white half-square triangles? _____

How many white squares? _____

What is their finished size? _____

What is their cut size? _____

How many single red triangles?
_____

What is their finished size? _____

What is their cut size? _____

How many large green triangles?
_____

What is their finished size? _____

What is the cut size of the square?
_____

Large side triangles

How many are there? _____

What is their finished size?
_____

What is the cut size of the square?
_____

Corner squares

How many are there? _____

What is their finished size? _____

What is their cut size? _____

Once you know all your unit requirements, you can figure the yardage you need for each color. We sincerely hope that this is getting easier and easier and you are starting to see how these blocks are drafted and where the measurements come from. The more you try this on your own, the closer you will be to looking at a photo and being able to translate it into a pattern with your own measurements and proportions. How liberating is that!

Once your top is finished, play with borders, settings, expanding the size, and so forth. This star is especially attractive when set on point as the center of a medallion quilt. You might want to keep going with this one and turn it into a larger quilt.

Now on to the real Feathered Stars with diamond points.

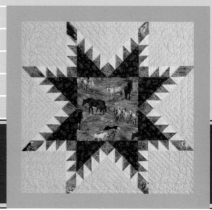

Class 380

Feathered Stars

Feathered Stars are one of Harriet's very favorite patterns, and she is not alone. They are often referred to as the grande dame of pieced quilts. There are dozens of variations, and they are all so different, yet the foundation of each of them is the same. The centers of the stars can be almost any shape or block. The most notable feature of Feathered Stars is the small triangles that make the "feathered" edging along each of the points. These small triangles are where the difficulty in drafting and piecing the pattern happens. You need to know if the two sides of the large triangle that the small ones will be sewn to are the same length. If they are different lengths, they may require two different-size triangles to make the edges fit exactly. You will find that the difference can be ⅟₁₆″ or ⅛″ per triangle square between the two positions. When you sew four of these triangles together, you can come up with ¼″ difference for the total side. This can be a huge problem for fit if the triangles are not paid careful attention. You encountered this a bit in Class 370 with a couple of the mock Feathered Stars: two different-size half-square triangle units. They appear the same size, but the ⅛″ dif-

ference is a big deal. Piecing Feathered Stars should not be difficult for you at this stage of your course work, but it is time-consuming. We are introducing 45° diamonds, getting you ready for Volume 4. There are also two methods for piecing these blocks, one using set-in corners and one using partial seams. We will walk you through one of each.

Remember, these blocks cannot be rushed. That being said, the quilt top you will be making in Lesson Two is accomplished in a seven-hour class in Harriet's Academy classes at her store. The students prepare the half-square triangle units and precut the pieces before class, and by the end of the day, their quilt tops are complete. The most gratifying thing to the students is that they honestly don't think they can pull it off—they are not skilled enough—and they wear ear-to-ear smiles of accomplishment at the end of the day to see that the time, precision, and care they have put into learning to be precision piecers has paid off. For the teacher, that is what we wait for—the sense of accomplishment coming from our students. We sincerely hope you will have that same elation and will share your success with us by sending photos of you and your achievement.

LESSON ONE:
Drafting Feathered Stars

Before we delve into the workings of Feathered Stars, we want to acknowledge Marsha McCloskey for being the premier Feathered Star expert. Her book *Feathered Star Quilts,* copyrighted in 1987, was and still is the definitive work on Feathered Star quilts. The gallery in the front of the book is awe inspiring, and the book is one of the only sources for endless Feathered Star patterns that always work. It offers a beautiful variety of all the basic types of Feathered Star blocks. The book concludes with complete drafting information for the different types of stars. For anyone who really wants to pursue Feathered Star quilts, we highly recommend classes with Marsha and getting a copy of the book. Although the book is out of print, used copies are out there for you to hunt down—ISBN 0-943574-34-X. Once you get Feathered Stars under your belt, Marsha has two newer, more advanced books available—*Feathered Star Quilt Blocks I* and *Feathered Star Quilt Blocks II.* Visit www.MarshaMcCloskey.com for inspiration, patterns, and books by Marsha.

There are three basic eight-pointed geometric stars in patchwork. Feathered Stars are created when you border the points of these stars with small triangles. Two of the stars are based on grids, which we walked you through in Class 350. Variable Star is based on a nine-square grid, and the Sawtooth Star is based on a sixteen-square grid. The third star is based on the LeMoyne Star, which is not a grid but a circle of eight 45° diamonds that make the points of the star.

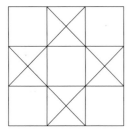

Variable Star

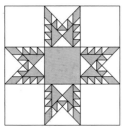

Joining Star

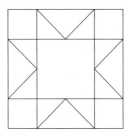

Sawtooth Star

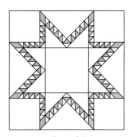

Feathered Star

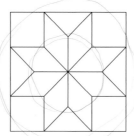

LeMoyne Star

Radiant Star

We are going to illustrate the step-by-step process of drafting a Feathered Star block, but this is by no means a complete set of directions for drafting all the stars you might see. Again, we defer to Marsha for the technical, mathematical, and detailed instructions you need to really learn to draft these patterns. We are merely introducing you to the process. This will let you get inside the design and truly understand it. We hope that you are starting to see the drawback to computer-aided design programs. Yes, it might be easier up front, but your brain doesn't learn the true workings of anything if it doesn't go through the step-by-step process of truly learning the hows and whys of the process. Drafting and design is truly the best part of quiltmaking, although over the past fifteen years we have lost much of the knowledge of being quiltmakers. We have been taught to rely on the work already being done for us, and we just sew. We applaud you for pursuing this amazing craft with us.

These blocks require graph paper that is larger than 8½″ × 11″. If you cannot

find large sheets of graph paper, tape smaller sheets together to get the size you need. We recommend 17″ × 22″ of ¼″ or ⅛″ graph paper. Also, have a sharp hard lead pencil and eraser, a drafting ruler (we prefer the C-Thru B-85 ruler), a bow compass with a 7″ radius, and colored pencils.

Feathered stars are generally drafted from the inside out. You will not know the outside dimensions of the block until you draft the inside. Make sure you draw the lines very accurately. We identify the template pieces if you choose to use templates to cut. Otherwise, use them to arrive at the rotary cut measurements needed.

We have chosen a star based on the nine-patch grid Variable Star. Once you have the basic star drawn, you can play with creating different centers or changing the block's orientation on point.

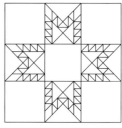

Variable Star

We are basing the feathers on a 1″ scale. That means the triangles are 1″. You do not know how big the block will turn out to be, but you do know that the feather is 1″ on its short side. If you look closely at the block, you see 3 feathers along the long side of the larger triangle. Therefore, that line, the hypotenuse (the longest side of a right triangle, opposite the right angle), must be 3″ long. A row of 1″ feathers lies on both sides of this 3″ dimension: 1 + 3 + 1 = 5, so 5″ is the length of the side of the center square.

1. Draw a 5″ square (Unit 1), extending the lines beyond the square. Don't worry about how long to extend them. They can be added to or erased later.

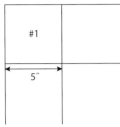

Drawing 5″ square with extended lines

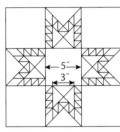

Joining Star

2. Draw lines 1″ inside of and parallel to the extended lines, as shown.

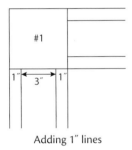

Adding 1″ lines

3. In this 1″-wide column, draw 3 – 1″ squares (Unit 3). Divide the squares in half on the diagonal to make feather units.

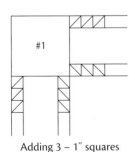

Adding 3 – 1″ squares

4. Draw diagonal lines that begin at the A points and end at the B points, as shown (Unit 2).

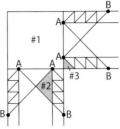

Draw in diagonal lines.

5. The feathers that fit the short side of the #2 triangle will be a different size from Unit 3. Find the midpoint of the short sides of the #2 triangles, as shown. On ¼″ graph paper, that line passes diagonally across 6 – ¼″ squares. Simply count down 3 diagonal squares (half of 6) to find the center. Using the graph paper as a guide, draw diagonal lines that begin at the midpoints and run parallel to the short sides of the #2 triangles. The square that is created is Unit 4. The parallelogram at the tip is Unit 5. Draw 2 more #4 size squares, as shown, and divide them in half to make Feather Unit 6.

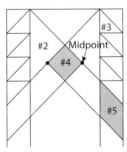

Finding midpoints

6. The side triangle (Unit 7) is made by connecting the tips of the #5 parallelograms.

7. The corner square (Unit 8) measures 5½″ on each side and can be completely drawn for that dimension. To get the finished size of the block, add 5½″ + 5″ + 5½″. That gives you 16″. You now know the finished size of your Feathered Star block.

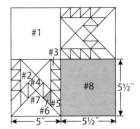

Finding measurements

Now have some fun changing elements within the star.

Color the units differently.

Change the orientation of center square.

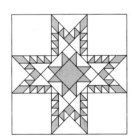

Add a pieced block to center square.

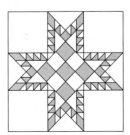

Change the scale of the center square.

Also, think about turning the block on point. This new orientation changes the name of the block to Star of Chamblie. Once the block is on point, play with changing the center, as shown on previous page.

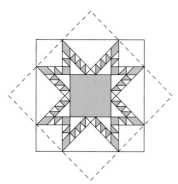

Put the block on point.

Now that you see the inner workings of the block, are you ready to try your hand at one? We are starting you off with the larger quilt top. This is the same pattern used in our classroom with great success. Take your time and work accurately each step of the way, and you will gather the reward in the end. Have fun!

> *tip* Once you get into drafting your own blocks, you will no doubt come up with 1/16" increments in some of the pieces. This is where the Feathered Star Ruler by Marsha McCloskey is indispensable for cutting. It is marked with both 1/8" and 1/16" lines, making accuracy much higher.

When designing quilts from scratch, you often need a specific size block. There is another way to draft these stars knowing what size they will end up being, and all the half-square triangles are the same size. Stay tuned for more.

LESSON TWO:
34" Feathered Star—Carrie's *Western Star*

This is a large star that will make working with so many pieces a bit easier for your first experience with a Feathered Star. This star introduces you to set-in piecing by setting-in two of the large outside triangles at the end of the construction process.

Western Star

Start by preparing all the pieces you will need. Being organized and well prepared is a major help when constructing these more complicated blocks. We suggest you mark on the backside of each piece the corresponding letter and whether it is a reverse cut (diamond only). Use the illustration of the star to identify your fabric color choice and placement and to identify the appropriate letters given in the cutting instructions.

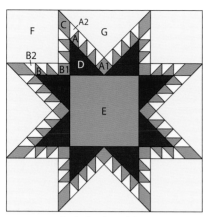

Basic Feathered Star

Yardage:

Fabric 1: ¼ yard (points [C] and large inside triangles [D])

Fabric 2: ½ yard (center square [E])

Fabric 3: ½ yard (background [F and G])

Fabrics 4 and 5: ½ yard each of 2 fabrics for half-square triangle units (A and B), squares (A1 and B1), and single triangles (A2 and B2)*

Note: The darker fabric is for the feathers, the lighter is the background. This can be the same fabric as the background, but it is fun to make this choice a bit lighter or darker than the background above.

As you cut out the pieces, be sure to mark on the back of each piece the corresponding letter above. Once the half-square triangles are made, mark them also, as the 2 sizes are only ⅛" different in size, and they are very easily mixed up. Keep all the pieces in separate envelopes so they are safe until you are ready to use them.

Cut:

Fabric 1: (Units C and D)

4 – 6⅞" squares. Cut each square in half diagonally. (We will explain in detail later how to cut the diamonds from this fabric [C].)

Fabric 2: (Unit E)

1 – 12½" square

Fabric 3: (Units F and G)

4 – 9½" squares

1 – 17¼" square; cut in half diagonally twice.

Fabrics 4 and 5: (Units A, A1, A2, B, B1, and B2)

4 – 2⅝" squares of feather fabric (A1)

4 – 2½" squares of feather fabric (B1)

4 – 3" squares of light fabric, cut in half diagonally (A2)

4 – 2⅞" squares of light fabric, cut in half diagonally (B2)

Construct 24 – 2⅝" (cut size) half-square triangle units using the feather and lighter fabric (A), using your favorite method.

Construct 16 – 2½" (cut size) half-square triangle units from the above strips (B).

> *note* Remember to mark the backs of the units made with fabrics 4 and 5 with the appropriate letters—A, A1, A2, B, B1, and B2. The ⅛" difference in size between these two letters can cause you much frustration if they get mixed up.

To cut the diamonds, you will be working with a strip that is folded wrong sides together. This will give you 1 and 1 reverse for each cut. You will need to cut 4 diamonds, 2 layers thick.

Cut 2 – 2⅝"-wide strips of fabric 1. Keep the strips folded in half. Using a long ruler with a 45° line marked on

it, cut 1 end at a true 45°. Keeping the 45° line on the long cut edge of the strip, move the ruler down until the 2½" line is on the angle cut at the end of the strip. These are not true diamonds, as they are shorter than wide. Make your second cut at this point. Continue until you have made 4 cuts. That will give you 4 and 4 reverse diamonds.

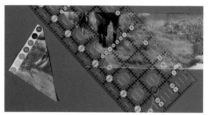

Position of ruler for cutting diamonds

Lay each individual diamond on top of the template at the end of the chapter and mark of the wrong side of the fabric the A and B shown on the template to denote which side is which. Because one side is shorter than the other, you will need to know which side goes to the A triangle and which side to the B triangle during construction.

Separate the diamonds. Lay them face down into 2 piles so that the A and B sides are the same within each pile.

Backs of pieces marked with correct letters

Remember—accuracy, accuracy, accuracy!

CONSTRUCTION STEPS

 hint Get organized. Save confusion and time by laying out the units on the table on the right side of your machine in the proper arrangement according to the diagrams. Be sure all the pieces are oriented correctly and enough pieces are in place. Do this with each step. Stack up the pieces two deep so that they stay in the correct order.

1. Join one B1 square, two B half-square units, and one B2 triangle, as shown below. Press the seams toward B1 and B2. Press the center seam between the half-square units open. Add one D triangle. Press toward D. Make two and two reverse.

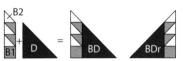

Constructing short side of feather

tip Speed sewing tip: Stitch two pairs of half-square triangles together—cut the back one off, bring it to the front, and add the square (B1). Cut the back unit off again and add the square. Cut the back one off and add the triangle to the opposite end (B2); repeat for the back one again. This eliminates a lot of wasted time and wasted thread. It can also help you keep the seams accurate and the placement correct. Before cutting the thread when these units are finished, start again on the reverse sets. Cut away the first sets once the first two pieces of the reverse set are started.

tip Piecing tip: When attaching the B units to D, have the B unit on top of the larger D triangle. Align the square end exactly. The point of the triangles on the other end should align at exactly ¼". Stitch, making sure you intersect the triangle points of the B units exactly.

2. Join 3 A half-square units. Chain sew as in Step 1. Press the seams open. Join one A2 triangle to one C diamond. Be sure to sew the triangle onto the A side of the diamond. Align the edges carefully. Press toward the diamond. All edges should align perfectly. Sew the diamond unit onto the half-square triangle units. Make 2.

Attach both to a G triangle, using the same technique as in Step 1. Press toward the G triangle. The points should align perfectly. Check for accuracy of the points along the seam.

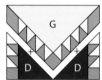

Attaching A units to G triangles

3. Join three A half-square triangle units and one A1 square. Press the seams open on the half-square pieces. Press the last seam toward the square. Join one A2 triangle onto a C diamond. Press toward the diamond. Attach these units to the other side of the G triangle from Step 2. Press toward G.

4. Join two D units to a G unit. This will be the first time you have to create a perfect intersection at the diamond. Position carefully. Hand baste if necessary to align the points and then stitch the seam. You might want to machine baste using longer stitches to test the points. If they are spot-on, restitch with shorter stitches. If they are off, the stitches are easy to remove. You have six points coming together at one place—a bit tricky. If you have been super precise up to this time, these points can naturally align correctly. Don't let it frustrate you if they don't come together easily. Patience is a virtue, and precise points at the diamond are critical.

Combining the D and G units

5. Join two B half-square triangle units. Attach a B2 triangle to the B side of the diamond. Join both pieces together into one strip. Construct two and two reverse. Join these units onto square F. Check the diagram for proper placement.

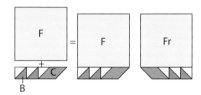

Constructing the F corners

6. Connect one F unit and one F reverse unit onto the sides of one unit made in Step 4. Do this twice.

Joining units together to create top and bottom of star

7. Join three A half-square triangles, one A1 square, and one A2 triangle. Make 2. Connect these units to the bias edge (long side) of the remaining D triangles.

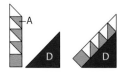

Using remaining D triangles

8. Join three A half-square triangles and one A2 triangle. Check the illustration for orientation. Attach this long strip just at the end—the half square onto the square that is already attached to the D triangle. Stitch only as far as the stitching line. This will allow the seam allowance to remain free so that we can set-in a large triangle later. Do a tiny backtack at the seamline. Do this twice.

Adding second row of feathers

9. Add the bias edges of the remaining D triangles to each unit, as shown. Do this twice.

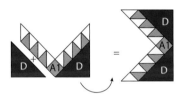

Adding second D triangle

10. Join the two units pieced in Step 9 to opposite sides of the E square.

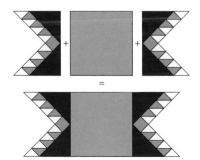

Adding sides to center square

11. Attach the rows constructed in Step 6 to the center row you just completed in Step 10. One will be the top of the star; the other will be the bottom row. Find the center point of the center square and pin the small square of the first row exactly into position.

Be careful to butt the seams of the center and align the points of the diamonds and triangles. Stitch the rows in place.

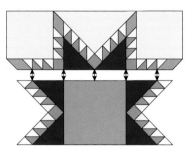

Lining up all points of each seam

12. Set-in the remaining G triangles. The seam allowance was left open to help this process. Pin one side of the triangle in place. You might need to lay the quilt top out of the way so that you can gain access to the seam you left open in Step 8. Sew from the raw edge of the seam allowance and the triangle. Start at the inner seam and stitch out toward the diamond edge. Repeat for the other side, flipping the quilt top out of the way so that you can position the other side of the triangle into the inner corner. Pin securely. Sew from the corner out toward the diamond. Press the seam allowances toward the G triangle.

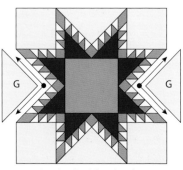

Setting-in side triangles

Give yourself a big pat on the back and take yourself out to dinner! What an accomplishment—you should be very proud! Add borders and you are ready to quilt, or save this to be a center for a medallion quilt in Volume 5. Are you ready to try a smaller star?

Carrie's Note

I decided to make this quilt to go in one of the rooms in my house and a square quilt just wasn't going to work. You can see that with a little bit of graph paper work I have added borders and two rows of blocks to make my quilt rectangular, and now it is a lap quilt in my den. The first border around the Feathered Star itself is made up of 17 – 2" half-square triangle units per side. There is then a 3½" border all the way around the quilt, and then I added the two rows of blocks. I had never made either of these two blocks before and thought this would be a good opportunity. There are a total of 14 Variable Star and Ohio Star blocks, each 6", in the two rows, separated by 1" spacers. The final border was cut 7" wide and was trimmed to 5" after the quilt was quilted. If you too don't want a plain square Feathered Star block, play around with it on graph paper and see what you can come up with—or set it aside and use it as the centerpiece of one of the medallion quilts you will design in Volume 5! Have fun!

Using partial seams—Star of Chamblie

It's now time to scale things down a bit and work with small triangles. You will find the 1″ size of the half-square triangles requires careful measuring and patience. We are going to piece this block with the method Marsha McCloskey teaches, called halfway, or partial, seams. This method is basically the same process as is used with the 34″ star, but there is no setting-in of the last two large triangles. Four side units and four corner units are constructed and then joined easily because some seams are not sewn to the end. This block will be 15⅜″ when completed. There are ¹⁄₁₆″ measurements in this block, so cut very carefully. Take your time and measure with every step, and this block will be fun to make. If you get anything off at any step, it goes downhill fast. Consider this a check-in point for your precision skills—and patience! Once you have made one of these, we hope you will enjoy it so much you are inspired to make a few more and design a quilt top to show off your accomplishment. Have fun!

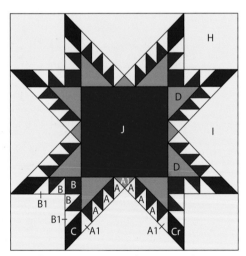

Placement of star elements identified
with letters

We are not listing colors in the cutting directions, as we want you to color in the above diagram to determine where you want different colors to be positioned. Add the color names to the cutting directions if that helps you keep the colors straight. The directions below are for a 2-color block.

You will need:

24 – 1½″ square half-square triangle units (A)

8 – 1⁹⁄₁₆″ square half-square triangle units (B)

Star of Chamblie

(These can be made from a 10″ square of both the light and dark fabrics, cut into 2″ strips if you choose to use the bias square method.)

Cut from light fabric:

4 – 1⅞″ squares, cut in half diagonally (A1)

4 – 1¹⁵⁄₁₆″ squares, cut in half diagonally (B1)

1 – 9″ square, cut in half diagonally both directions (I) (Consider cutting this square a bit larger to eliminate the problem of the side not being straight in the end.)

4 – 4¹⁄₁₆″ squares (H) (Consider cutting the squares a bit larger.)

Cut from dark fabric:

2 – 1⅞″ squares, cut in half diagonally (A1)

4 – 1⁹⁄₁₆″ squares (B)

2 – 4¼″ squares, cut in half diagonally both directions (D) (Consider cutting the squares a bit larger.)

1 – 6⅜″ square (J)

1 – 1½″-wide strip. Keep the strip doubled, wrong sides together. Make a 45° cut at one end and move your ruler down 1⁹⁄₁₆″. Cut 4 diamonds. You will have 4 and 4 reverse (C). Be sure to mark on the wrong side of each diamond the A side (the 1½″ side) and the B side (the 1⁹⁄₁₆″ side).

CONSTRUCTING THE BLOCK

This time we are going to avoid set-in seams by using partial seams. The following diagrams will have brackets that indicate seams that are partially sewn at the beginning of the construction process and completed later. Because you are working with very small pieces, we recommend that you lay out all the pieces for both the corners and the side units so that you can be sure you have all the parts and that the colors and positions are correct.

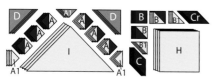

Layout of all pieces

1. Start by constructing the side units. The instructions will be for one unit—you will need to make four. These can be made at the same time, or one first to test your accuracy, and then the other three. Position one triangle I, six A half-square units, two light and one dark A1 triangles, and two D triangles as in the illustration above.

2. Join three half-square units in a row, making sure the dark triangles are pointing in the correct direction.

> *tip* We suggest that you measure each unit you sew together as you go to ensure that the measurements are staying accurate. When you sew the three A half-square units together, press the seams open and measure. This unit should measure 3½". If it doesn't, check your seams and correct.
>
>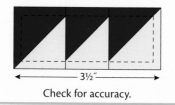
>
> ← 3½" →
>
> Check for accuracy.

Once these units are pressed and measured, add the A1 single triangles onto one end of each. Again, check the illustration carefully to make sure you get the angle in the correct position. Press this seam open. Sew this row onto the I triangle with a partial seam. Stitch from the square corner to the second half-square unit. Press the seam toward the I triangle.

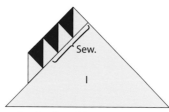

Sewing first side onto I triangle

3. Join the remaining three half-square units in a row, adding an A1 triangle at the end. Notice that this side is turned the other direction from the opposite side.

Sew this row onto the opposite side of the I triangle with a partial seam. Stitch from the square corner to the second half-square unit.

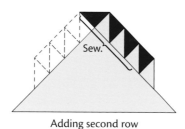

Adding second row

4. Add the D triangles to the outside edges of the half-square rows, as shown below.

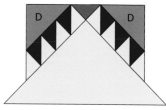

Adding D triangles

> *tip* Be sure that when you add this triangle, the points are extended beyond the ends of the row of feathers by ¼". Once the triangles are added and pressed, the points in the center of the unit at the single red triangle need to be exactly ¼" from the raw edge. Measure this unit and be sure all the points are right on and the corners are square.

5. Repeat Steps 1–4 to make a total of 4 of these units.

6. For the corner units, which were laid out above, start with one H square, one each C and C reverse diamonds, two B1 single triangles, two B half-square units, and one B square.

7. Start with one half-square unit, one B1 triangle, and the C reverse diamond. Stitch the diamond onto the single triangle and press the seam allowance open. Be sure that the 1⁹⁄₁₆" side of the diamond is sewn to the triangle. Add the half-square triangle to this unit. Press the seam open. Make 4 of these units. Sew these strips onto one side of the H squares. (See the diagram.) Press toward the square.

Joining B1 triangle to diamond

Half-square units for corner

8. Sew one B half-square unit and one B square together. Press the seam open. Sew a B1 triangle to a C diamond, making sure the 1 9/16" side is the edge you join to the triangle. Press the seam open. Join this unit onto the half-square triangle. Make 4 of these units. Add these units to the remaining corner of the square.

Joining B1 triangle to diamond

Second side added to square

9. Lay out all of the pieces. You should have 4 corner units, 4 side units, and the center square. Start by sewing the corner units onto the sides of the center units in the top and bottom rows.

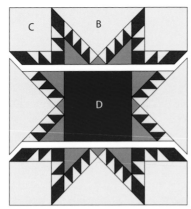

Block layout

This is the first time you will encounter aligning the diamond points. There are six points coming together in one spot here, so careful alignment is crucial. You can try to do this visually or use a pin to position the points. Carefully push a pin straight through the points on one side and then insert it into the points of the other side. Keep the pin straight up to pull the points together. Pin on either side of this pin and then remove the positioning pin before stitching. Don't be surprised if you have to rip this out a time or two until you find the perfect way to pin to achieve accuracy.

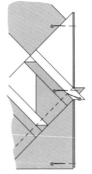

Positioning pin

Once the first seam is sewn, press toward the feathers. Complete the partial seam and press toward the large triangle.

10. Sew the side units onto two sides of the center square. Watch the two points in the center of the seam. They need to be sharp and precise. Press toward the side unit.

11. Sew the top section to the center section, sewing the long seam first. You again have the diamond and feather points to match. Finish by completing the partial seam on either end. Repeat for the other side of the center.

Once the block is pressed, measure from the point of the diamonds out 1/4" on all sides to square the block.

We hope precision piecing is getting easier and easier for you. We also hope you love this block so much you are willing to do several of them and create a wonderful Feathered Star quilt—they are true showstoppers and will blow away your quilting friends! Now sit down with a cup of tea and pat yourself on the back, looking at your work with pride. You have come a long way from learning to sew an accurate seam. Are you ready for the Final, for the last of the quilts in Volume 3?

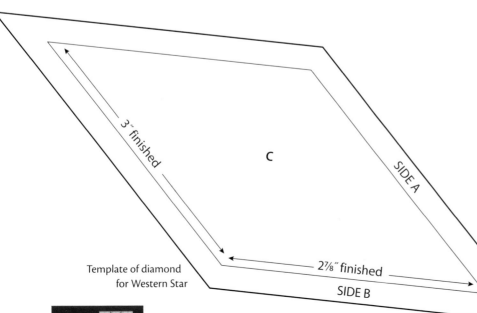

Template of diamond for Western Star

Class 390

Prairie points

We chose this edge finish for Volume 3 because it is totally triangles all around the edge of the quilt. Prairie points are a fun way to add interest to the edge of a quilt. You can use many different scraps as with Method One or Two, or use only one or two colors if you use the continuous method. Choose the method that suits the look of the quilt.

Instead of a binding, this is an inserted edge finish. An inserted edge can include prairie points, scallops, ruffles, or piping. An inserted edge is attached to the front and the batting by sewing through both layers all the way around the quilt. The back is then folded over the seam allowance and blind-stitched in place. Prairie points can be added after the quilt top is quilted—especially if the quilting extends to the edges of the quilt top—or even before the quilting is done.

METHOD ONE

This is the traditional way of making points. It is accomplished by using small squares of fabric and folding them into triangles. These triangles are overlapped and sewn to the edge of the quilt in place of a binding.

To determine how many prairie points you need for each side of your quilt, use this formula. Take the length of your quilt, then divide by the finished base of a single prairie point, and multiply by 2. For example, if you are making a 45″ × 60″ baby quilt, the length is 60″. So 60 ÷ 3 = 20 × 2 = 40 prairie points for each side of the quilt. The top and bottom sides are 45″. So 45 ÷ 3 = 15 × 2 = 30 points needed for the top and for the bottom. You will need to make 140 prairie points for the quilt.

To determine how big you want the finished prairie points to be, take the height of the finished point × 2 + ½″. That equals the size square to cut. If you want 2″ finished prairie points, you would use this formula:
2 × 2 = 4 + ½″ = 4½″ squares.

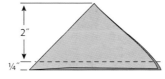

2″ x 2″ = 4″ + ½″ = 4½″ cut square
Figuring the size to start with

Use the following instructions to create your prairie points.

1. Fold each square in half diagonally, right side out. Fold in half again, forming a small triangle. Press.

Folding a prairie point

2. Working from the quilt top front, align the long side of the folded triangle to the raw edge of the quilt top. The points will be facing in toward the quilt top. Begin at the center of one side of the quilt. Nest the points one inside the other, as shown below. Adjust the amount of overlap to fit the side of the quilt you are working on and pin securely in place. At the corner, have the long edge of one prairie point start right on the raw edge. Stitch it onto the quilt top and batting.

Nesting points on edge of quilt top and batting

METHOD TWO

The second way to create prairie points for the edge of your quilt is to fold the square into a rectangle, wrong sides together. Press. Make 2 diagonal folds into the center to create a triangle that has a vertical line. Press it flat.

Folding square into a rectangle

Overlap the prairie points on top of one another, as shown in the illustration. The points cannot nest with this method. Adjust the overlap along the edge of the quilt until the prairie points all fit evenly.

Overlapping points along edge of quilt

Prairie points are usually added after the quilting is completed. Trim the batting and backing to be even with the edge of the quilt top. Fold the backing away and pin it so that it cannot be caught when sewing the edge. Starting at one corner, sew the prairie points to the quilt top and batting using a ¼″ seam allowance.

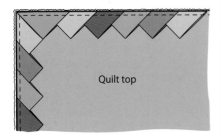

Sewing points to edge of quilt

Once you have sewn all four edges, trim out as much of the batting from this seam as possible. This will eliminate the bulk caused by the extra fabric from the triangles. Turn the prairie points so that they face out from the quilt top. The raw edge of the quilt top will be inside. Turn under ¼″ of the backing. Blindstitch the folded edge of the backing to the prairie point edges, completely covering the seam.

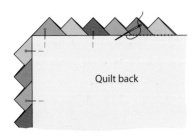

Stitching backing over seam

A very slick way of making continuous-band prairie points has been floating around since before 1989, but the name of the inventor and its place of origin seem to have been lost. It has been in magazines, given out as free handouts by sewing machine companies, and offered in guild newsletters. Whoever came up with this great idea, we really appreciate it!

There are fewer possibilities for variation in color and fabrics with this method than with the individual squares, but it's certainly faster and easier. Because the prairie points are not made individually, they are always the same size and evenly spaced.

To determine the size of the strips for your prairie points, take your desired height of the prairie point plus ¼″ × 4.

ONE-COLOR PRAIRIE POINTS

Our example here will produce an edging with triangles that finish to 1¾″ high: 1.75 + .25 × 4 = 8″. As always, we recommend that you make a sample to experience the technique and determine what your measurements will be.

1. Start by cutting an 8″-wide strip of fabric the same length as one edge of the quilt, plus about 6″ extra. If necessary, piece strips together to get this needed length.

2. Place the wrong sides of the strips together and fold the strip in half lengthwise. Press well.

3. Place the fabric strip wrong side up, opened to the 8″ width. Beginning at one end, start marking off 4″ segments on one side of the

band. On the opposite side, begin 2″ in from the end and again mark off 4″ segments. It makes no difference if one side is longer or has more squares than the other.

4. Cut the squares on the marked lines from the outer edge to the center pressed fold.

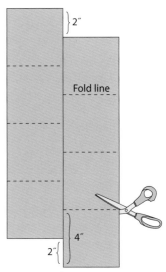

Prepare 4″ segments on strip.

You will be pressing as you go, so work at the ironing board. Begin by turning the fabric wrong side up and fold the points as follows:

a. Beginning with Point 1, place it nearest to you and make the first fold, as shown. Next, turn the top corner down for the second fold.

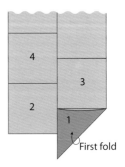

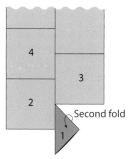

Begin folding process.

b. Move to Point 2 and make the first fold. Next, fold Point 1 across the bottom part of Point 2. Make the second fold of Point 2. This will enclose half of the base of Point 1. Pin in place.

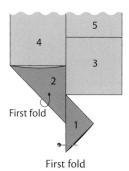

First fold

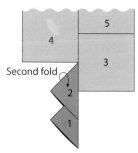

Fold Point 1 across bottom part of Point 2.

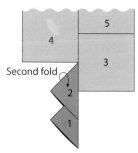

Fold Point 2.

c. Next, make the first fold of Point 3. Now fold Points 1 and 2 over and make the last fold on

Point 3. This will enclose half of the base of Point 2. Pin in place.

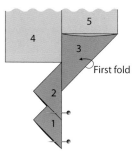

First fold of Point 3

d. Continue in this manner, alternating from side to side, until all the points are folded and pinned.

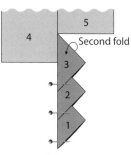

Fold Point 2 across bottom part of Point 3.

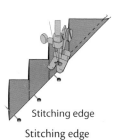

Fold Point 3.

5. Once the entire strip has been folded and pinned, machine stitch ⅛″ from the raw edge, removing pins as you go. Press.

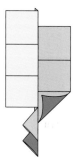

Stitching edge

6. Repeat this process for each side of the quilt.

TWO-COLOR PRAIRIE POINTS

Two-color prairie points are constructed the same as above but work with 2 strips, each a different color.

1. Start by cutting 2 strips, 1 each from different fabric. To determine how wide to cut them, use this formula: finished height × 2 + ¾″. For this example, we want 2″ finished points, so 2 × 2 + ¾″ = 4¾″.

2. Instead of folding a wide strip in half, you will be sewing the 2 different strips together, wrong sides together with a ¼″ seam. Press to the darker strip and starch lightly.

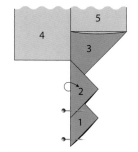

Working with 2 colors

3. Lay the strip on the table with the seam allowance down and the wrong side up. Mark (4½″ squares this time), cut, fold, and press as described for 1-color prairie points.

4. Pin the prairie points in position on the right side of the quilt top, keeping the backing fabric out of the way. If there are any extra complete points beyond the edge of the quilt, cut them off. Do not cut through a point. Ease if necessary to make it fit the length of the edge.

5. Sew a ¼″ seam allowance through all the layers except the backing. Trim any excess batting close to the stitching.

6. Once the prairie points have been sewn, fold them away from the quilt top and stitch the backing in place along the seamline on the back using a blind or ladder stitch. (These stitches were taught in Volume 1, Class 190, page 105, and Volume 2, Class 290, page 104.)

LESSON TWO:
Choosing batting for your new quilts

One of the most overlooked, least understood, and least discussed products in quiltmaking is batting. This key ingredient can either enhance a quilt's beauty or detract from and distort the quilt's surface. No one batting is appropriate for every quilt. Quilters must consider factors such as desired surface texture, weight, warmth, loft, drape, shrinkage, fiber content, washability, bearding properties, ease of needling, and so forth. All of these factors play as important a role in a quilt's overall appearance as do fabric choices, design piecing, and the appliqué techniques. Remember, a top is not a quilt until it is quilted, and batting makes a top a quilt.

Machine quilting adds another dimension to your batting choices. As a beginner, you want to use a batting that will cooperate with you and your machine to eliminate distortion and thus frustration. As your skills improve, so will your willingness to take on more unruly battings and larger quilts. The fiber content, manufacturing process, and loft of each different batting will affect the manageability and success of the quilting process.

There are many excellent battings on the market, but there is no one perfect batt. If you feel very confused by all the different battings available, don't feel alone, as most of us have a hard time keeping up with all the new products that continually appear. At the time of this writing, there are over 110 different battings on the market. Many of them are actually the same batting from the same factory with a different brand name on the package; but nonetheless, you have to sift through an awful lot of product to discover what is truly appropriate for your new quilt top. Unfortunately, most quilters have access to only a handful of different types and brands.

Harriet worked with the Hobbs Bonded Fibers Company for more than twenty years, developing new battings that were user friendly and would produce superior quilts. Among her top products are 80/20 Premium, 100% Wool, and Tuscany Silk. One of the hardest jobs was to educate salespeople on why batting is not all created equal and the finished product is more important than the raw product—meaning the texture, weight, and softness (cuddle quality) of the quilt after it is washed is more important than the tactile properties of the batting. A quilter's ability to sandwich and handle the quilt layers while quilting also is reflected in the way the batting is manufactured.

Harriet has heard for years that machine quilting makes the quilt stiff, or that the nylon thread used by many machine quilters causes this problem, when actually it is the bat-

ting and how it is finished. If you have a heavily needle-punched batting, it will obviously be stiffer when quilted than an open, delicate batting. Today's quilters have been sold on the softness of the batting and the ability to quilt 6″ or more apart, not on softness of the finished quilt. We see people pet batting, thinking the softer the fiber feels, the softer the quilt will be. Think about it—you will never pet the batting again once it is in between two layers of cotton fabric, so how can the tactile feel of the fiber really make a difference? Instead of petting batting, examine how the batting is made. If it is like a blanket, the quilt will be flatter, stiffer, and not very warm. If the batting is lightweight, loose in fiber, possibly even able to be torn, and a bit puffy, the quilt will finish to be softer, more pliable, and warmer. Warmth is retained from heat being caught in the loft of the fibers—dead air space. That is why polyester and wool are warm—not only because of the fiber, but because the batts are thicker (not heavier). The more you quilt on these two battings and flatten them out, the less warm they will be as quilts.

The fiber content of the batting will affect the look and feel of any quilt. Cotton, polyester, and wool are the most common batting fibers. There is a trend today, however, to create boutique battings—battings made from trendy fibers like corn, bamboo, soy, and believe it or not, green recycled plastic! When asked why these products are being put on the market, the answer Harriet has received is "because we can." Do you really want to sleep under a plastic quilt? And we thought polyester was hot! Bamboo is broken down the same way wood pulp is to produce the fiber, therefore making it exactly like rayon. There are few environmental benefits to the harsh chemicals used in this process, making it not such an earth-friendly product. Corn and soy are food sources, so do we really need to be taking those products and making batting? Trends are one thing, but the added expense of the products is not justified by what they don't deliver. Cotton, wool, polyester, and silk are every bit as good and have certainly stood the test of time in hundreds of years of quiltmaking history. As you start to investigate batting brands and fibers, don't get caught up in the latest marketing scheme. Keep to the look and feel of the end product to make your final decisions.

Terminology can get rather confusing as we talk about different types of battings, so we are adding a short list of definitions to clear things up a bit.

Bearding This refers to the migration of fibers through the quilt top or backing fabric. Don't confuse bearding with puncture marks. Puncture marks occur when a dull or too-large needle pushes the batting fibers through the backing fabric in the needle hole. Hand quilters can also experience this with some battings if they use a rough thread or too much beeswax on the thread. The fibers of the batting can be dragged through the needle hole on the thread. True bearding will look a bit like shedding. Polyester is the biggest culprit, and the fibers will migrate to each other, causing pills to form on the top of the fabric. Wool can beard slightly, but after a couple of washings, this usually stops, as the fibers intermingle with one another because of the barbs on the fibers themselves. Low thread count fabrics are also a

big problem with polyester and wool battings.

Cotton breaks off at the surface of the fabric and seldom if ever has a problem with bearding.

Bonding Bonding is the process that is used to hold batting fibers together to prevent fibers from shifting and migrating. Two different processes are used:

❋ *Thermal* Low-melt polyester fibers are combined with wool, polyester, or cotton fibers and heated by means of an oven, radiant heat, or an ultrasonic wave. The temperature is high enough to melt the low-melt fibers but not the other fibers in the batting. When the fibers melt, they cling to the other fibers, causing bonding points.

❋ *Resin* A light coating of resin or glaze is sprayed on both sides of the fiber web. It is then heated in an oven to dry and cure the batting. Resin-bonded battings generally have a higher, lighter loft that is easier to quilt through.

Carding This process takes the fiber from the bale and turns it into a web. A rotating drum with barbs on its surface separates and combs the fibers into a web. This web can be used without any further treatment. Early cotton quilt battings were webs of carded cotton placed between two pieces of paper. The batts needed to be quilted ¼"–½" apart to prevent the fibers from shifting. The quilts that used these batts were very soft. Today the web is then either cross-lapped, needle-punched, and bonded, or any combination of the three.

Loft The thickness of the batting is referred to as loft. It can also refer to the resilience of the fibers over a period of time.

Needle-punched This mechanical process uses boards of embedded

barbed needles that intermingle the fibers. As the batting web moves down the line, the needle boards pierce the layers and interlock the fibers into a fairly tight product. This is felting, or the making of a nonwoven fabric. The more needles or the slower the batting passes through the machine, the more tight and heavy the needling is. You will see various weights and thicknesses of these battings on the market.

Scrim This is a very thin, sheer layer of polypropylene, similar to a lightweight interfacing. It is an added layer to the batting web that is then needle-punched to one or both sides of the batting. Scrim lets you quilt farther apart but can have a hard and fairly stiff surface. These battings are not the best choice for bed quilts but do work well for craft products like place mats, table runners, jackets, and so forth.

TRADITIONAL COTTON QUILT BATTINGS

The most commonly used natural fiber in quiltmaking is cotton. As evidenced by antique quilts, cotton stands the test of time. Whether you desire a batting that reacts like those products available in the 1800s or 1930s, or you want the more contemporary look of the new products, both are available. Vintage-style cotton batts require closer quilting (1″ and closer) and will have a higher percentage of shrinkage than the newer needle-punched batts that can be quilted up to 3″ apart. Claims are made that if a scrim binder is added, you can quilt up to 8″–10″ apart!

Cotton is still king in the batting market. More battings are made using cotton than any other fiber. Here are some of the characteristics of cotton that accommodate the needs of today's machine quilters.

❊ The cotton fibers of the batting stick to the quilt top and backing fabrics, preventing the shifting, slipping, distortion, and stretching that occur with polyester battings under the machine. This allows us to pin baste less, and eliminates puckers, tucks, and ruffled borders on our machine-quilted quilts.

This is the major reason for a beginning machine quilter to use cotton battings.

❊ Because the fibers do stick together and the batting is much thinner, when the quilt is rolled to go through the sewing machine, the roll is much smaller.

❊ Most cotton battings shrink some when washed. The shrinkage is generally at the same rate or higher than the cotton fabrics used in the quilt top. Shrinkage can be beneficial for several reasons:

It gives the quilt an aged look, which is desirable when trying to replicate an antique quilt.

When you are just learning to machine quilt, there are glitches in your work that you want to camouflage. The shrinkage of the batting, when the quilt is first laundered, causes puckering around the stitching. This makes it difficult to tell how the quilt was quilted and hides many of the little problem areas. This helps you learn faster, as you can quilt on your small quilt tops instead of spending hours practicing on muslin.

❊ Cotton is extremely comfortable to sleep under. Cotton breathes, allowing excess heat to escape. It makes excellent baby quilts.

❊ Cotton endures. Even with hard use, cotton ages gracefully, becoming softer and cuddlier with age.

❊ Pure cotton battings do not beard.

Brands available:

❊ Mountain Mist 100% Natural Cotton

❊ Mountain Mist Blue Ribbon

❊ Fairfield Cotton Classic 100% Organic Cotton

❊ Mountain Mist Cotton Blossom—A Touch of Natural Luxury

NEEDLE-PUNCHED COTTON BATTINGS

Needle-punched cotton batting became available as a craft batting in the early 1990s. It was intended for wall quilts and craft products but soon became a staple for quilts because of the 6"–10" distance between quilting lines that was advertised. The first of these products had a scrim binder added during the felting process. This seemed very appealing to quilters who didn't want to quilt the traditional cotton battings that required 1" or closer stitching. Many brands are now available, often the same product in different packaging produced at the same factory for different batting companies. Much like fabric production, one factory will make the same product—with a few minor differences—to be sold by several different private labels.

The softest and most drapable of the needle-punched battings are the ones without a scrim binder. They can be a bit more fragile and stretchy and might not be the best choice for wallhangings. We suggest that none of these battings without scrim be quilted farther apart than 3", although the packaging will state 4"–6". The more the quilt is quilted, the more durable it is. This is where these battings fall into trouble, as the more you quilt them, the flatter and stiffer they get. When selecting one of these battings, compare the amount of needle-punching and the denseness in several brands. Don't get caught up in the softness of the fiber. This has nothing to do with the end product!

note *Many batting brands suggest that they can be quilted up to 10" apart. We would like you to be aware of a basic problem with this misleading claim. What is being said is that the batting will not fall apart if quilted up to 10" apart. However, those making the claim are not taking into consideration the weight and wear and tear on the limited number of quilting stitches that are expected to hold everything together. Quilts are heavy and even heavier when wet during washing and drying. When a quilt is quilted farther apart than 3", there are not enough quilting lines to support this weight. This causes broken stitches and quilts that wear quickly and look less than healthy in a very short period of time. We would like you to consider keeping your quilting lines no farther apart than 3" when planning your quilting design. If you look at the beautiful antique quilts that have survived for the past 150-plus years, you'll notice that they are heavily quilted, especially compared to many of the quilts that have been produced in the last 20 years of quiltmaking. If you want your labor of love to last through years and years of use, try to avoid the temptation of taking the easy way out and doing minimal quilting on your tops. With good batting choices and adequate quilting, your quilts should look lovely for a long, long time.*

Brands available without scrim:

* Fairfield Poly-fil Natural 100% Cotton
* Fairfield Soft Touch 100% Bleached Cotton
* Hobbs Heirloom 100% Natural Unbleached Cotton
* Hobbs Heirloom 100% Bleached Cotton
* Hobbs Tuscany 100% Unbleached Cotton
* Hobbs Tuscany 100% Bleached Cotton
* Mountain Mist White Rose
* Mountain Mist Cream Rose
* Pellon Legacy 100% White Cotton
* Pellon Legacy 100% Natural Cotton
* Quilters Dream 100% Cotton, Request, Select, Deluxe, and Supreme
* Warm Company Soft & Natural

Brands with polypropylene scrim:

* Air-Lite Colour Me Cotton 100% cotton with scrim
* Airtex 100% Natural Cotton
* Airtex 100% Bleached Cotton
* E.E. Schenck Co. Nature's Best Cotton
* E.E. Schenck Co. Nature's Best Bleached Cotton
* Fiberco Simply Cotton
* Fiberco Simply Cotton Bleached
* Hobbs Heirloom 100% Natural Unbleached Cotton (Craft Cotton)
* Hobbs Heirloom 100% Natural Bleached Cotton
* Pellon Legacy 100% White Cotton with Scrim
* Pellon Legacy 100% Natural Cotton with Scrim
* Warm Company Warm & Natural
* Warm Company Warm & White

COTTON/POLYESTER BLENDS

Fairfield started blending polyester with cotton in 1979, and by the 1990s, blending became quite the trend. Blending fibers together can give the advantages of both fibers in the product. The polyester and cotton blends are some of today's most popular battings. The polyester adds a bit of loft to the cotton, making it lighter and easier to hand quilt as well as warmer. The most common blend proportion is 80% cotton and 20% polyester. You will see, however, a variety of proportions, and this can account for a vast difference in the behavior and feel of the batting after it is quilted. The numbers listed after the brand names below denote cotton first, polyester second; that is, 80% cotton, 20% polyester.

Brands available without scrim:

* Fairfield Quilter's 80/20
* Hobbs Heirloom Premium 80/20
* Hobbs Heirloom Bleached 80/20
* Mountain Mist Gold 50/50
* Warm Company Warm Bond 80/20

Brands available with scrim:

* Air-Lite Colour Me Cotton and Polyester 80/20
* Airtex 50/50 Cotton/Polyester
* Airtex 80/20 Cotton/Polyester
* Fairfield Machine 60/40 Blend
* Fiberco Soft and Elegant 80/20
* Pellon Legacy 80/20 Blend
* Warm Company Warm Blend 50/50

MISCELLANEOUS BLENDS OF DIFFERENT FIBERS

The latest trend in battings is to blend unique fibers together to get various results. We call these boutique battings, as they are generally hard to find, and the price is usually quite a bit higher than cotton and cotton/polyester blend battings. Below are some of the combinations available.

Brands available:

* Pacafil 50/50—50% alpaca/50% cotton with scrim
* Pacafil 60/40—60% alpaca/40% wool with scrim
* E.E. Schenck Co. Nature's Best— 50% bamboo/50% organic cotton with scrim
* Fairfield Nature-Fil Bamboo— 50% bamboo/50% cotton with scrim
* Fiberco Soft Soy Blend— 50% cotton/50% soy with scrim
* Hobbs Tuscany Silk—90% silk/ 10% polyester, no scrim
* Mountain Mist Cotton Blossom Wool Blend—95% cotton/5% wool, no scrim
* Mountain Mist Cotton Blossom Silk Blend—95% cotton/5% silk, no scrim
* Mountain Mist EcoCraft Eco-Friendly batting—50% PLA/50% cotton (corn derivative), no scrim
* Mountain Mist EcoCraft Eco-Friendly batting—50% soy/50% cotton with scrim
* Pellon Legacy Bamboo Blend— 50% bamboo/50% cotton with scrim
* Pellon Legacy Soy Blend— 50% soy/50% cotton with scrim
* Quilters Dream Orient—bamboo/ silk/cotton botanical Tencel blend, no scrim

As you can see, the list seems endless! Many of these battings feel and look just like 100% cotton battings once quilted. Make sure you see and feel a quilted sample, or make one of your own before investing the higher price for these battings. You might be just as happy with a tried and true cotton batting that has been around for a long time.

100% WOOL

Harriet worked with Hobbs Bonded Fibers in the 1990s to bring out the first machine-washable quilt batting made of 100% wool. You might ask— why wool? Wool is the fiber of choice when warmth and durability are needed, and we now use it as a substitute for polyester when natural fibers are desirable. The comfort of wool is universally recognized as superior to man-made (plastic) fibers. It is warm and lofty without being heavy but can be quilted extremely close without getting stiff and hard. Wool quilts are a cut above most others.

Wool has characteristics that no other fiber provides. First, the wool fiber has built-in crimp, giving it bounce and loft that allows it to always return to its original shape. Wool has a recovery rate from compression of 95 percent, which is better than any other fiber. (Polyester averages 73 percent, depending on the type of polyester fiber treatment used.) This resiliency provides long-lasting beauty and warmth.

Wool batting provides superb insulation. The interlocking fibers breathe, allowing excess heat to disperse from the body. This allows our skin to remain warm yet dry. It moderates temperature, so you never get too hot or too cold when sleeping under it. Wool gives warmth without weight. It is naturally hydroscopic and can absorb up to 33 percent of its own weight in moisture without feeling damp, as opposed to 4 percent for synthetics and 8 percent for cotton. This makes it a perfect quilt for a damp, cold climate. Polyester tends to become clammy when damp.

Wool is naturally flame-resistant. When exposed to flames, it smolders at a low temperature and self-extinguishes with a cool ash,

making it an extremely safe fiber to use for small children.

A concern many have concerning wool is mildew and insect damage. When it is between two layers of cotton fabric—the top and the backing—wool does well. Moths do not eat cotton, so they cannot get to the wool if it is totally covered. In addition, moths do not eat wool fibers unless dirt—their food—is attached to the fibers. The fibers are damaged as the moth eats the dirt. You can protect your quilts, as well as any other wool items, by keeping them clean.

High-quality wool battings are made from preshrunk fibers. This keeps the fibers from shrinking when the quilt is washed. There will be a slight shrinkage amount in all wool battings. Be sure to dry your quilt in the dryer until just damp dry, then remove it and lay it out flat to dry. Drying your quilt bone dry will cause the fibers to shrink, and it will take some time for them to relax and lie flat again. By laying the quilt out flat just before it is completely dry, the fibers are relaxed, and the quilt retains the soft loft.

Brands available:
❋ Fairfield Nature-Fil 100% wool—light acrylic resin bonding
❋ Hobbs Heirloom 100% wool—light acrylic resin bonding
❋ Hobbs Tuscany 100% wool—light acrylic resin bonding
❋ Quilters Dream 100% wool—thermal bonded

THE BATTING TEST

Now you probably feel totally confused and overwhelmed by the number of different battings available—and we didn't cover them all! Don't feel alone, as most of us have a hard time keeping up with all the new products that continually appear. Remember, confusion is the beginning of knowledge! We suggest that you obtain samples of, and thoroughly test, every batting you can get a piece of and every new batting product that appears on the market. If you will take the time to do the tests below, you will know everything you need to make your quilts have the exact look you want, and you will know how they will age, how close you need to quilt them, and so forth. You truly have no valid excuse not to do these tests if you want to be a true quiltmaker. The information you glean from them is invaluable.

First, collect 3 – 14″ squares of every batting you can find. If you have trouble obtaining a variety of batting samples, please contact us at www.harriethargrave.com. We have sample packs available just for this testing process.

note *Please do not prewash any batting. Battings are not stable enough to withstand being wet, then dried. Uneven shrinkage, tearing, and stretching are a few of the problems you will encounter if you try to wash a batting. If shrinkage is a concern, you will be able to see the look of the batting after it is quilted, washed, and dried after the samples are completed.*

Next, create a pile of 14″ squares of high-quality muslin (quilt-shop quality only) that is prewashed and a pile that is unwashed. Label the squares with a permanent marker to identify those washed and unwashed. In the center of each of these squares, draw a perfect 6″ square with a permanent marker. These squares will be the tops of the blocks.

For the backing squares, sew a 7¼″ strip of black cotton to a 7¼″ strip of muslin. Cut into 14″ squares. You will need a pile of these made from preshrunk fabric *and* a pile from unwashed fabric.

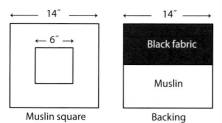

Preparing the top and back squares

You are now ready to layer the batting and fabric together. Do so in the following order:

1. One piece of unwashed batting with unwashed fabric—top and back.

2. One piece of the same unwashed batting with prewashed fabric—top and back.

Label the muslin square with the following information: the brand of batting and whether the fabric is prewashed or not and any other information you feel is pertinent—like when the batting was purchased.

You should have one square of unwashed batting left. Make a copy

of the sample sheet at the end of this Class for every brand and type of batting you are testing and staple the remaining batting square to it. Use it as a control sample for future comparison against new batts of the same brand to compare for consistency. If you find that the batting looks and feels different from the one you tested, you may want to run a new test on the new batt to see if it will perform differently from the original.

Now you will need to quilt the samples. If you are a hand quilter as well as a machine quilter, hand quilt half of the block and machine quilt the other half. On the form, make a note of whether you enjoyed quilting this batting and which method you preferred. If you are not a hand quilter, simply machine quilt the entire block. Quilt within the distances that are given on the package, or to your liking, never quilting farther apart than 3″.

This is an excellent time to experiment with various threads and needles. The rayon, metallic, and cotton embroidery threads will react differently to different battings. Work out the machine tension settings and problems here, instead of on your quilt. Also experiment with the various needles available to see which type and size give you the best results on your machine. Use these batting samples to learn as much as possible. Also, note any tension adjustments that were needed for that particular batting, or differences in tension setting for various types and brands of threads and needles. Stitch-length settings and preferences can also be noted for each batting.

Once you've quilted it, measure the 6″ square. Using those measurements in the following formula, compute to see if you have lost any size from quilting (known as contraction). Many battings will cause a size loss in the finished size of the quilt simply from the take-up that occurs in the quilting process.

$$\text{\% of shrinkage} = \frac{\text{original} - \text{final}}{\text{original}} \times 100$$

Make a note of any size changes. Finish the edges by serging or zigzag stitching.

Once you have done this, it is time to wash and dry the quilt blocks. Wash and dry them the way you would care for your finished quilts. Once the blocks have dried, organize them so that the samples of the same brand of batting are together. Look at them and start to form your own opinions. Is one sample too wrinkled and another too flat? Do you really like the sample with the unwashed fabric and unwashed batting, but the prewashed fabric and unwashed batting did not work out too well? Start to eliminate the combinations that distort the blocks or just don't appeal to you. Be aware of your feelings toward the look of the sample. You will find that you may like one combination, but your best friend prefers another. This is okay. Quilting is a very personal skill, and we should be making quilts that appeal to us and look like what we like, not just trying to please everyone else. If you like the finished result—go for it! It's your quilt.

Next, remeasure the 6″ square in the center of the block and rework the shrinkage formula. This gives you the total amount of size loss due to contraction and shrinkage from washing and drying. Now you can use these findings to determine if you need to make your quilt top a bit larger than the finished quilt needs to be, based on how the batting performs. Shrinkage doesn't need to be feared; learn about it instead and make it work for you.

The reason for the black on the back is to help look for bearding problems. Are tiny fibers migrating to the surface of the fabric? Are many fibers migrating? If so, this batting would not be a good choice for dark fabrics. Also, look at the top of the block. Is the dark color shadowing through the batting to the top of the block and discoloring (appearance only) the top surface? This is a typical problem with polyester batting. It also dilutes the color of lights, making them appear slightly gray or tired looking. Cotton battings are opaque, and light cannot pass through them. You will not see the color coming from the back to the top on a cotton batt because of this. The cotton also keeps the true color in the top fabric by providing a "backing" that light cannot penetrate to dilute. If you want to put a dark backing on a light quilt top, you can if you are wise in your batting choice.

Once you have filled out the form, wash and dry all the samples again. Continue to do this week after week. Make a mark on each square every time it is washed and dried.

Examine the samples after five washings, again after ten washings, and so forth. After ten to fifteen washings, see how the batting is holding up. Is this a batting you could use in a baby quilt and wash weekly, if not daily, and have it hold up? Alternatively, is it fragile and not aging well under such use? Determine where and when these battings would be appropriate in the quilts you make. Not all quilts lie on closet shelves, but not all quilts are on kids' beds either.

Now you have the start of a batting library. Before you start a new project, look through the batting samples before you buy the fabric and/or do anything with it. As you look through the samples, ask yourself these questions about your new quilt:

* Do I want natural fiber, synthetic, or a blended batting?

* Do I want it thick or thin?

* Do I want it flat or fluffy?

* Do I want to hand quilt it or machine quilt it?

* How close do I want to quilt this quilt?

* Do I need this quilt for warmth, or do I want a cooler quilt—is it for summer, spring, fall, or winter temperatures?

* Is the quilt going to be washed a lot, or is it just for show?

* Is the quilt going to hang on the wall or lie on a bed?

* Do I need the quilt to look antique or contemporary—should it be smooth or pucker?

If you can answer all these questions for every quilt you make, you will be matching the appropriate batting to every quilt top you make. This information is not available in a quilt book or classroom. The only way to truly learn about batting is to do the samples. We know that most of you won't do the samples. You will probably say that you don't have time to waste on muslin samples. However, you do have the time and money to invest in a quilt top that you love, only to be disappointed in the results because the batting does not look right.

Think about it this way—as you get further into the art of quilting and start practicing various machine-quilting techniques, you will need samples to practice on. What if you were to spend some time to collect the ingredients and layer them together as suggested above? Then when you sit down to practice your quilting skills, you already have the practice pieces ready. Instead of throwing away your practice blocks, you set them aside to test. As you practice, you are not wasting an hour of time, an ounce of batting, or a yard of fabric. You are learning to quilt, and you are developing an invaluable reference library of brands and types of battings, as well as what combinations they can be successfully used in and how well they wear with repeated launderings. What else could you ask from just a few hours of preparation and practice?

Batting sample test sheet

Brand name: _____

Fiber content: _____

Sizes available: _____

Recommended quilting distance: _____

How did it needle? _____

    Hand: _____

    Machine: _____

Thread used: _____

    Top: _____

    Bobbin: _____

Needle used: _____

Appearance after quilting? _____
_____
_____

Bearding? _____

Shadowing through? _____

Contraction when quilted? _____

Shrinkage after washing? _____

Opinion of appearance after washing:

Which combination did I like best? _____
_____

Appearance after 5 washings: _____

    after 10 washings: _____

    after 15 washings: _____

Quilts I have used this batting in: _____
_____
_____
_____

Other comments: _____
_____
_____
_____
_____
_____
_____
_____

SPLICING

Battings come in many sizes, but often you need a larger size than is available in a particular brand, or you want to use up large pieces of the same product that you have leftover from other projects. This is when you will need to splice two batting pieces together. It is common to butt two straight edges and whipstitch them together. The problem with this method is that the splice will appear as a "break line" through the quilt, especially as the quilt ages. Harriet suggests overlapping the two pieces of batting 6″–8″. Cut a serpentine line through both layers. The gradual undulating curves will butt together perfectly once the end of each layer is removed.

6″–8″ overlap

Cut a serpentine line through both layers.

Hand stitch the batting together using ½″-long loose herringbone stitches. This serpentine-stitched splice will eliminate any unsightly evidence of where you made the splice.

Herringbone stitch

LESSON THREE:

Quilting design ideas

You will find that the quilting patterns and techniques are starting to get a bit more complicated and technically more difficult. We are still keeping the skill level as beginner, but it is more advanced beginner at this stage. Carrie has been quilting all of her own tops through these books, and we are trying to keep the techniques within her comfort range. We are using Carrie's progress as a gauge for how other beginners will be progressing as they work through the books. You won't learn to quilt if you don't try, and you will probably find that it is not nearly as hard as some people let on, and what a star in your crown when you can declare that you did it all yourself! Again, we strongly suggest that you use Harriet's book *Heirloom Machine Quilting*, 4th Edition, as a workbook. It is written as a class manual and is the text for her hands-on classes.

Happy quilting!

Vintage Broken Dishes

Poinsettia Table Runner

Sampler

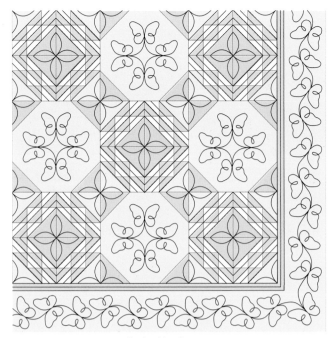

Spring Has Sprung

Prairie Windmills

Log Cabin Basket

Yankee Puzzle

Homeward Flight

Cat Tracks and Bird Trails

Beachy Snail's Trails

Amish Baskets

Winter Goose Chase

Sawtooth Star

Western Star

Colonial Star

Goose in the Pond

Your Junior Final

If you have worked through this entire book, you should be very proud of yourself! Triangles can be a bit trying, as there are several steps that are necessary to make them extremely accurate and to have points spot-on when sewn. The quilt that we have chosen for your final for this volume incorporates many of the processes you have learned from Volume 1 through Volume 3.

Unlike the other two finals we have put you through, this one will be a bit different. We feel that if you have worked through all three volumes of the Quilter's Academy series, you have the knowledge and skills needed to make this quilt. The techniques used in this quilt are:

❋ Strip piecing—Rail Fence blocks and Nine-Patch blocks

❋ Half-square triangles

❋ Flying Geese

❋ Template drafting and cutting

❋ Precision piecing

The center unit is easy enough, so the pieces will be in the breakout format for you to figure out, using the grid size and the individual units needed. The corners, on the other hand, are rather complex and use templates and precision piecing. Therefore, we are going to include the templates and give you some instructions as to the order to piece the units together in. Take your time and walk through it piece by piece.

We suggest that you draft out the elements on graph paper so that you understand how the pieces fit together and can double-check the templates we are giving you for this quilt. You might want to make it into a larger size, and by drafting it, will have the templates sized to your specific needs.

Good luck with this one. It is a good challenge.

Goose in the Pond

GOOSE IN THE POND WORKSHEET

Quilt top size: 39″ square

Grid size: 1″ (smallest unit)

Center square:

Rail fence units—1″ grid

Nine-patch units—1″ grid

Half-square triangle units—3″ grid

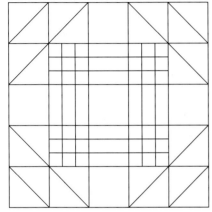

Center square unit for *Goose in the Pond*

Breakout of center unit

Half-square unit

How many half-square units are in the center square? _____

Which method would be most efficient to construct half-square triangles? _____

First plain square

How many squares of this color are needed? _____

How many inches of strip will be needed? _____

Second plain square

How many squares of this color are needed? _____

How many inches of strip will be needed? _____

Nine-patch unit

How many nine-patches are needed? _____

How many inches of strip sets will be needed? _____

Rail Fence block

How many units are needed? _____

How many inches of strip sets will be needed? _____

CORNER UNITS

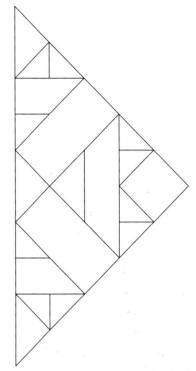

Corner unit

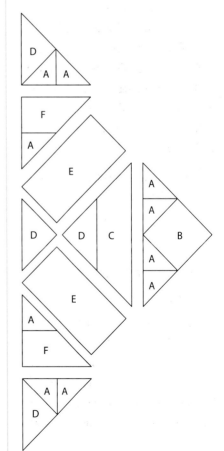

Corner unit breakout

Unit A

How many Unit A's are in each corner? _____

How many are needed for all four corners? _____

Unit B

How many Unit B's are in each corner? _____

How many are needed for all four corners? _____

Unit C

How many Unit C's are in each corner? _____

How many are needed for all four corners? _____

Unit D

How many Unit D's are in each corner? _____

How many are needed for all four corners? _____

Unit E

How many Unit E's are in each corner? _____

How many are needed for all four corners? _____

Unit F

How many Unit F's are in each corner? _____

How many are needed for all four corners? _____

FIRST BORDER

How many running inches are needed of the rail strip set for the four sides of the quilt top center? _____

How many additional running inches of strip sets are needed for the four corner Nine-Patch blocks? _____

FLYING GEESE BORDER

How many geese are needed total? _____

Which method would be the most efficient? _____

CORNERS OF FLYING GEESE BORDER

What units are needed for the corners? _____

CENTER DIAMONDS

Templates provided

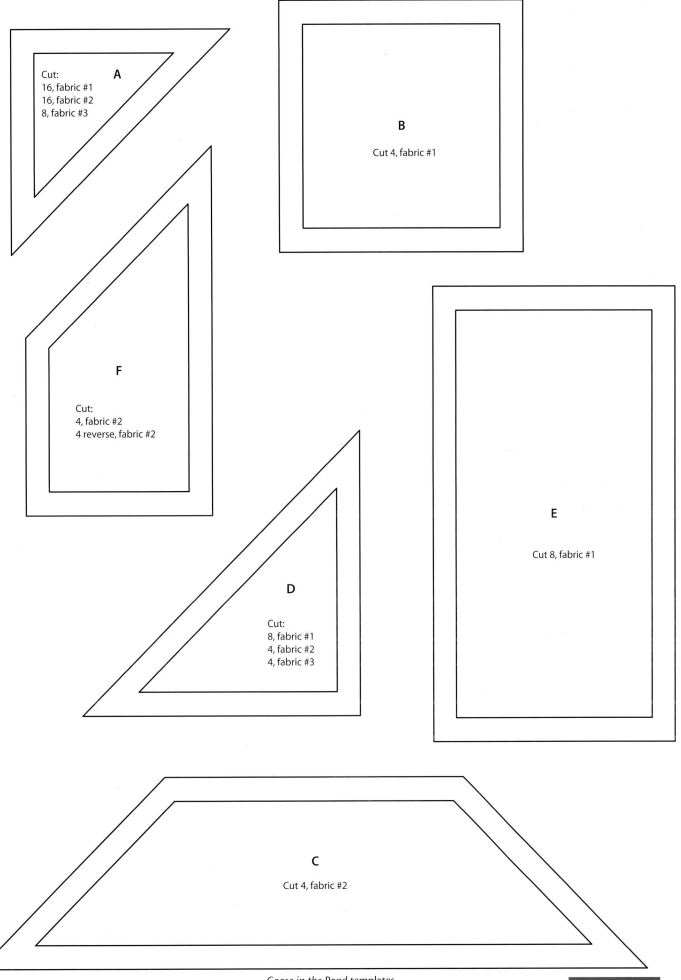

A
Cut:
16, fabric #1
16, fabric #2
8, fabric #3

B
Cut 4, fabric #1

F
Cut:
4, fabric #2
4 reverse, fabric #2

E
Cut 8, fabric #1

D
Cut:
8, fabric #1
4, fabric #2
4, fabric #3

C
Cut 4, fabric #2

Goose in the Pond templates

About the Authors

Harriet started quilting seriously in 1974, working alongside her mom. Her early quilting career included producing baby quilts for craft shows and teaching adult education classes. In 1981, Harriet opened her quilt shop, Harriet's Treadle Arts. Her specialties at the time were free-motion embroidery, machine arts, and machine quilting.

In 1982, Harriet attended one of Mary Ellen Hopkins's seminars. Mary Ellen's streamlined techniques and innovative design ideas led Harriet to a new way of thinking, which caused her to give up the machine arts and to teach only quilting.

Today, she is world renowned for being a true "mover and shaker" in the quilt world. In the late 1990s, she was voted one of the "88 Leaders of the Quilt World."

Harriet created and inspired a whole new generation of machine quilters with her best-selling book *Heirloom Machine Quilting,* which has enjoyed 22 continuous years in print. She is also the author of *Mastering Machine Appliqué* and *From Fiber to Fabric,* and co-author of *The Art of Classic Quiltmaking.* She is responsible for a myriad of products pertaining to machine quilting, and she has developed batting with Hobbs Bonded Fibers and designed fabric for P&B Textiles.

Carrie has been around quilting all her life—sitting in Harriet's lap as a baby while Harriet sewed, learning her colors with machine embroidery thread and her alphabet on the cams of Harriet's old Viking sewing machine. She didn't have a chance not to be involved! Harriet and her mother opened the store when Carrie was four years old, and she spent a part of nearly every day of her life at the store. Carrie's interests in college turned to range management and wildlife biology, but no matter what, she always came home to quilting as a hobby.

In 2006, Harriet decided she wanted to close the store. She was tired after running it for 25 years as well as traveling and teaching at the same time. Carrie couldn't imagine not having the store as a part of her life. So she moved back to Colorado and now runs the store full-time.

Most of all, Carrie is proud to carry on the family legacy of quilting that extends from her great-great-grandmother Phoebie Frazier, to her great-grandmother Harriet Carey, to her grandmother Harriet (Fran) Frazier, to her mom, Harriet. Quilting is all about tradition (no matter how you make a quilt) and about the love of creating something beautiful from fabric and thread with your own hands.

All the quilts in the book were pieced and quilted by Harriet and Carrie. They truly believe that if you are going to teach it, you had better be able to make it!

Resources

SUPPLIES/SOURCE LIST

All notions and supplies referred to in the text are available from the following:

Harriet's Treadle Arts
6390 West 44th Avenue
Wheat Ridge, CO 80033
303-424-2742
harrietstreadlearts@earthlink.net
www.harriethargrave.com

Information on Harriet's classes, retreats, and conferences can be found on her website.

If you are looking for copies of Harriet's out-of-print books referred to in the text, they are available through C&T as eBooks and as POD (Print-On-Demand) Editions. Go to www.ctpub.com and search by author name to purchase.

We would like to thank Red Rooster Fabrics for supplying us with the fat quarter bundle to make Carrie's Star in Class 370 (page 95).

Other titles by Harriet Hargrave: